Marmalade Skies

Gus Gresham

This novel is a work of fiction. Any similarities with characters living or dead is purely coincidental.

Cautionary Note

At the time of publication, this novel was set 50 years ago. In the early 1970s, growing up was similar in some ways and different in others. The attitudes of parents and carers were often different, too. Some of the activities described in this story would be dangerous today (as they were in the 1970s). Always listen to the advice of a parent or carer, and ...
DON'T TRY ANY OF THIS YOURSELF.

for Sue & Bevan

1

Gallows Hill

It struck Vonnie again, during the Sunday dinner ritual, that no matter how hard she tried, she just didn't fit in. Not among girls. Or boys. Or even in this town. And she definitely didn't fit into her family, with her scaredy-cat mam and nutter of a stepdad.

"We'll be all right," Mam kept saying.

"No, we won't," Vonnie would say.

She'd heard an expression on some telly drama recently. *Borrowed time.* And that was how it felt – that she and Mam were living on borrowed time; that if they didn't escape soon, something really bad would happen.

Vonnie was getting up from the dinner table when her stepdad said, "Where do you think *you're* going?"

"A drink of water."

"Si' down. You should have thought of it earlier. I was in the middle of the story as well."

Bill Skinner's shirt sleeves were rolled up, his hairy forearms on display. He was hairy all over, except for his head; he regularly shaved off the patches that still grew there. When he was satisfied that Vonnie and her mam were ready to listen again, he carried on.

"Yeah, so everyone in the pub knows this Lefty bloke's got form. He were big an' all. Bigger than me. Covered in tats. 'You were looking at me funny then, weren't you?' he says. 'No, I weren't,' I say. 'You *were*,' he says. 'You were looking at me funny. I don't like people looking at me funny.' So I say, 'I weren't, mate, and I don't want no trouble neither.' Fair chance, you see. I give him a fair chance to let it go. But he's not letting it go. His mates are all watching, enjoying themselves. Then Lefty says, 'Do a disappearing act, pal. Before I deck you.' And he was really big. Built like the proverbial."

"You told us this one last month," said Mam quietly.

Yeah, and ten times over the years, thought Vonnie.

"What did you say?" said Skinner.

"What I mean ..." said Mam. "I just seem to remember you might have told us this story before. Not long ago."

Skinner picked up his beer glass, took a swallow, placed it down thoughtfully and gave Mam a long look.

"You trying to start another argument?"

"No, no. Course not, Billy."

"Good. What's for pudding?"

"Rhubarb crumble and custard."

"Right. Go and get it. No, wait. I'll finish first ... 'I don't want no trouble, mate,' I tell Lefty. 'I've ordered a pint; I'm waiting for my pint.' Then he just lamps me one. Swings his fist from right back here, like this."

Skinner got to his feet to demonstrate the moves.

"Lamps me straight in the kisser. I stagger back against the bar. A bit dazed. He's got a fist like a sledgehammer. He comes at me again. I dodge. Like this. Lefty punches again. Gets me round the side of the head. Did I say how big he is? He's really big. Course, all his mates and every other punter's thinking he can't lose. Thinking that Billy Skinner's gonna get a right pasting. So I let him use up some energy, and I keep skipping and dodging, looking for a weak spot. But Lefty ain't got no weak spots. He can't lose. Everyone knows that. Few of 'em might have been putting bets on, for all I know. But I'm dodging his blows and doing all this fancy footwork. Light on my feet in them days, I was. Linda Moore'd tell you about that – Quick Step, Gay Gordons; we did the lot. Could have been a boxer, I could. Take that Cassius Clay. I used to be just as good. Probably better. So now that I'm warmed up and doing all the footwork and the ducking and diving, Lefty can't hit me. I keep dodging his blows. Giving him the run around. Then somehow, against all the odds – *somehow*, I send a punch straight through his defences. *Bosh!* Like that. Then another and another. And their mouths – everyone in the pub's mouths are wide open. They can't believe what they're seeing. Billy Skinner. *Bosh! bosh! bosh!* And Lefty goes down like a sack o' dog turds."

"Vonnie's here," said Mam. "Language."

"What? She's heard worse than that. She'll hear it at her new school anyway."

There was a knock at the door.

"Who's that?" said Skinner, alarmed.

"I don't know," said Mam. "Shall I answer it?"

"No. It could be *any*body."

He went over to the front window and peered through the net curtains.

"Some bloke," he murmured. "What's *he* want?"

Mam stood from the table.

"It's probably only – "

"Shhh! I think he's coming to the window. Get down!"

Mam sat again.

"No – *down!*" said Skinner in a loud whisper. "Down!"

He dropped into a crouch under the window sill.

Automatically, Vonnie and Mam slid off their chairs and went onto all-fours on the carpet. They did their best to hide among the chair legs and table legs and the tablecloth that was hanging halfway down to the floor.

It was best to humour Skinner, or they'd really end up paying for it later. They almost never had visitors of any kind. He'd always made it clear that he didn't like anybody coming to the house, and he'd have nothing to do with the neighbours. He wouldn't have a telephone either.

A man in a suit and tie appeared at the window. The man knocked once on the glass, squinting as he tried to see through the nets, then strode off.

3

Skinner pressed his face to the corner of the window.

"Right," he said, standing. "He's gone next door."

He dusted his trousers off, then drew the heavy brown curtains across. The summer's day was blotted out. He turned to where Vonnie and Mam were still crouching among the table legs.

"Where's this rhubarb crumble, then?"

Mam fetched it from the kitchen.

It looked and smelled delicious with its golden biscuit topping and the rhubarb juice oozing up through the crust in places. Vonnie loved the smell of the fresh custard, too.

Mam set out three bowls and began to serve.

"Don't give none to her," said Skinner, with a nod in Vonnie's direction. "She's left half her dinner."

Vonnie considered what she'd pushed to the side of her plate: some pimply cabbage and a chunk of meat gristle. If she was made to eat it, she just knew she'd puke. She looked at Mam, but Mam bit her lips and looked away.

Mam and Skinner ate their pudding while Vonnie did her best to chew and swallow the cold cabbage. There was no way she could put that disgusting gristle in her mouth.

Twenty minutes later, everything except Vonnie's dinner plate had been cleared away. She'd lost count of how many times she'd been made to stay at the table like this. Skinner sat opposite her, reading the Sunday paper, his next bottle of Double Diamond in front of him. Mam was in the kitchen doing the washing up. Vonnie prodded at the gristle with her fork, and lost herself in the usual fantasy about leaving home. Jumping on one of the freight trains that slowed for the bend around Gallows Hill. Going wherever it took her. Free at last.

After another half an hour later, Mam came back into the front room and dithered about. She kept giving Vonnie little smiles that were supposed to be supportive and encouraging or something.

Finally, Mam approached the table.

4

"I was just thinking, Billy ..." she said.

"No you weren't," he said.

"What I mean is – "

"She's staying there till she's cleared that plate."

Skinner folded the newspaper and put it under his arm.

"I'm going to the bog," he said. "No funny business while I'm gone. Right?"

Mam pursed her lips and looked at the floor.

You're not even my real dad, thought Vonnie. Not that she could remember her real dad. They'd left him when Vonnie had been about two, and then he'd supposedly died peacefully in his sleep a few years later. But Vonnie knew the truth from overhearing Mam talking to someone in town. She'd asked Mam about it lots of times, and Mam flatly denied it. Basically, though, Vonnie's real dad *had* died in his sleep, but he'd been comatose from booze and choked on his own vomit.

"I just can't, Mam!" she said, low and urgent, as soon as the toilet door closed across the hall.

"I ate all mine, love," said Mam.

"I know, but – "

"A good joint of meat, that was."

"I know. The meat was okay. But this gristle ... Please, Mam. *Pleeease*. I just can't."

"It's not as bad as it looks. I ate mine. It's ... got a sort of creamy flavour."

"What? *Creamy?*"

A tear rolled down Vonnie's cheek.

"I hate him," she said. "Hate him. He's a pig."

"Vonnie ..."

The toilet flushed.

"Right, listen," said Mam, a sudden conspiratorial note in her voice. "Just don't dare say anything ..."

Her hand shot out and she magicked the gristle away, folding it into a tissue which then disappeared down the top of her flower-print dress. Vonnie's relief was quickly

5

followed by a fluttering in her chest as Skinner came back into the room.

"What's going on?" he said, heading to the table.

"Nothing," said Mam.

"Something," said Skinner.

"No. Really. I was just saying well done to Vonnie for managing to eat it."

A moment of deadly silence.

"If you're lying ..." he said.

"We're not," said Mam.

Skinner smiled thinly.

"You looked suspicious when I came in," he said.

"She ate it."

"Suspicious. Both of you did. Whispering."

"No."

"*You* – loitering near the table. And *you* – sitting there all sheepish. I'm not an idiot."

Another thing about Skinner was that he didn't use their names. He used other people's names, like "Lefty" in the pub-fight story earlier. So he used names to talk *about* people. But he'd never say "Vonnie" or "Brenda" when he was speaking directly to Vonnie or her mam. It was "you" this or "you" that, and sometimes it was difficult to work out which of them he meant.

"No, you're not an idiot, Bill," Mam said softly as she stroked a hand down his arm. "But she ate it. I watched her eat it."

"Well ... is that right?" he said.

"I ate it," said Vonnie. She looked him in the face, held his gaze and added, "It was nicer than I expected in the end. Sort of creamy flavoured."

"I'll ... get you some rhubarb crumble," said Mam.

Skinner watched Mam go and called out, "She'll have to have it cold then. Don't waste any gas re-heating it."

6

2

Girls Will Be Boys

A week later, on the last Saturday of the summer holidays, Vonnie sat in her bedroom reading a favourite book called *Lost Slavic Folk Tales*. Its title always made her smile. Even if the stories had been lost for centuries, she reasoned, but had been gathered together in a collection like this and printed, didn't that make them *found* rather than lost tales? Anyway, she didn't doubt that all the stories were probably good, but she'd only read one. Whenever she picked up the book, she'd open it in the familiar place at that same story.

It was called 'The Stone Mason's Daughter'.

The stone mason tried to teach Agata his trade, but she seemed to have no affinity for stone. The mother had died in childbirth, and the stone mason knew now that he would never have a son. He made sure that Agata had enough to eat and that their shack was in good repair and kept out the rain and the north wind.

She was dressed in boy's clothes and her hair was shorn off every solstice. Her only friends were boys, but at twelve years old, she was leaving childhood behind.

The stone mason worked hard and drank mead in the evenings. Agata was keen to learn her father's trade, just as her friends were learning their fathers' trades. Some were apprentice blacksmiths and others were apprentice cobblers. They were happy because they knew what they were going to be.

One day, Agata's father said, "Don't you like stone?"

"I love it," said Agata. "I love it because you love it."
The stone mason wrung his hands.
"But stone doesn't like you ..."

Vonnie stopped reading and went out.

Before long, she came across Nidge and his gang in Blackthorn Woods, and tagged along with them as they hatched another of their nutty pranks.

The sun's heat blasted down into the big clearing. Pale weeds grew from the cracked earth and insects peppered the air. Four boys carried Nidge in a ratty old leather car-seat. More boys followed. Some were stripped to the waist; some held staff-like branches.

Vonnie's sweaty legs were sticking to her jeans. Her scalp itched. She kept wondering why the boys all blindly did what Nidge said. He was skinny and not even tall. But there he was, sitting all official in the car-seat, sunlight flashing off his glasses as he was lowered to the ground.

Matt and Eddie forced a struggling boy forward and made him kneel in front of Nidge.

"I've not done nuffink," said the boy.

"Shut it," said Eddie.

"Yeah," said Matt. "We caught you having a waz in the den where we have our meetings."

"I didn't know it was your den, did I?"

"Shut it," said Eddie.

Nidge scowled at the boy for a second, then turned to Matt and said, "What's the punishment?"

Vonnie laughed to herself. This was just play-acting. She'd been with them when they'd cooked up the prank and then trawled the woods looking for a victim and a reason. She thought that Nidge and his gang were basically all idiots, and she was only hanging around with them because there was nothing else to do in Blackthorn, and because it was better than being at home. Anything was better than being at home. What would she do there? Help

Mam scrub the cooker? Or watch *World of Sport* wrestling on the tiny black-and-white telly? Skinner kept saying he was going to get colour. So what if he did? Saturday afternoons would still be dominated by his loud, obnoxious glee as Mick McManus or Jackie Pallo pummelled their opponents onto the ropes.

Vonnie hated fighting. Even pretend fighting like TV wrestling. Nobody would think it, though. She'd been in a scrap with a boy called Rick earlier, and it had ended when she'd given him a split lip. He'd been keeping his distance since. They respected that – a girl who could fight.

"The punishment," said Matt, standing to attention and smiling goofily, "is Rabid Dog."

A cheer went up from the gang. It was echoed by the spectators at the edge of the clearing, though they couldn't have had any idea about what was coming.

"Rabbit Dog?" said the boy. "What you gonna do?"

"*Rabid* Dog," said Matt.

"Yeah, *Rabid* Dog, you prat," said Eddie. He was short and stocky, with dark hair and an impish face. "Now shut your gob before I ram my boot in it sideways."

The boy was another reason Vonnie was still there. Fair enough, he *had* been peeing in one of the dens, but she was sticking around to make sure things didn't go too far.

"Rick," said Nidge, talking to the blond lad Vonnie had scrapped with earlier. "Where's Killer? You were supposed to be getting him."

"Yeah, soz," said Rick. "I'll go now. Back in ten minutes."

"Make it five."

Rick sprinted into the trees.

Although she'd been in a different class and hadn't had much to do with them, she knew Nidge, Matt and Winston a bit from the old school. On Monday, they'd all be starting at the secondary modern.

"What you gonna do?" said the captive boy.

Nidge gave him a sort of benevolent smile.

"We could always let you be in the gang instead."

"Uh?"

"Yeah," said Nidge. "What's your name?"

"Alan Wirrell." The boy's face glowed with gratitude and relief. "But everyone calls me Badger."

"How old are you?"

"Eleven."

"You can't be," said Nidge. "*We're* eleven. You only look about eight."

"I'm eleven," said Badger. "Cub's honour."

"Cub's honour!"

"I don't go no more," said Badger. "Am I in the gang?"

"Not yet," said Nidge. "There's a special initiation. A test of courage."

"Okay. What is it?"

Nidge looked at Matt and Eddie.

Matt yanked Badger's tee-shirt over his head and Eddie tugged at the boy's trousers.

"What you doing?" said Badger. "What's the initiation?"

"It's the same," said Nidge. "Rabid Dog. Punishment and initiation are the same."

Badger groaned.

More gang members moved in.

A minute later, Badger was lying spread out on his back in his underpants, restrained by a boy gripping each of his wrists and ankles. Vonnie was nearby, and at the edge of the clearing there were a few other girls. She thought it was probably only because of some unspoken code that Badger's pants hadn't come off.

"Will it hurt?" he said. "Will it take long? I'm supposed to be home at five – "

"Shut it!" spat Eddie, standing over him and waving a sheath-knife slowly from side to side, so that the bright light glinting off its six-inch blade fell repeatedly across Badger's face. "Shut it, or I'll cut your tongue out."

Bored with waiting for Rick to come back, some gang members lay about the ground. Others kept firing their catapults and sending stones ricocheting off tree trunks or slashing through the foliage.

Eddie knelt beside Badger, whispering things into his ear. Badger's eyes bulged in response.

Vonnie felt sorry for the kid. He *did* only look about eight, but she knew he was eleven. Like the rest, he'd been in his last year at the old school before the holiday.

"All right, Vonnie?" said Matt, edging towards her and trying to be friendly. "This is a right laugh, ain't it?"

"Not really," she said. "Bit stupid, if you ask me."

"Er ... well ..."

Then Rick arrived, his Great Dane virtually dragging him into the clearing.

"Soz it took ages," he said, panting. "Mam made me go 'round the shop for Brillo Pads. "

Killer pounced at the car seat, ramming his front paws into Nidge's chest. The dog's head loomed inches from his face and a long pink tongue lapped at him enthusiastically. His glasses spun into the air.

"Arrgh! Get the – get this thing off me!"

Matt helped Rick pull Killer away.

Another boy picked up Nidge's glasses.

"Right," said Nidge shakily. "Get on with it."

Rick produced a can of Chum from a brown paper bag. Matt squatted on the ground with the can and selected a blade from his Swiss Army knife. As soon as the tin was punctured, Killer sent up a chorus of barks and howls. Three boys were needed to restrain him.

Matt raked the dog food out of the can, and it splatted onto Badger's chest. When he started yelling, Eddie grabbed a sock from the pile of clothes, but Matt pushed Eddie's hand away before he could stuff the sock into Badger's mouth. Somebody began to beat a slow tempo on an oil-drum. Badger whimpered and thrashed. Matt used

11

his hands to spread the dog food over the boy's chest and stomach, and it squished up through his fingers.

"Put some round his goolies," said Eddie.

Matt ignored him, stepped aside and nodded to Nidge.

Vonnie's heart raced. She took a step forward.

Nidge raised his hand, then lowered it in a chopping motion. Killer was released, and he immediately straddled Badger and began gobbling up the meat.

The drumbeat rose to a louder, faster tempo. Shouts and cheers erupted. Gang members sprang up and down, made ululating cries, waved their fists. Eddie's eyes glittered as he circled dog and victim in a kind of sideways dance, hands on thighs, boots raising dust from the dry earth, rapt face jutting backwards and forwards.

A cloud passed over the sun.

3

Summer's End

After plastering the dog food over Badger, Matt stood back to watch with a mixture of grotesque delight and worry. He glanced at Vonnie again. If she thought what they were doing was stupid, why didn't she just get lost?

When Killer had finished wolfing up all the meat, he went to work with his tongue, slurping, slurping, until Badger's body glistened, clean and white. Matt started to relax, remembering that Killer was, after all, just a big old softie. Then to his surprise, Badger laughed.

"It tickles," he cried.

"Right, he's in," said Nidge. "Let's go. Matt? Matt?"

"Yeah, coming," said Matt, though he hadn't moved.

In his peripheral vision, he saw that Nidge was being hoisted up in the car seat again, and that Badger was getting dressed. Vonnie had now walked off in a different direction. She'd surprised Matt and the others earlier by smacking Rick in the mouth. All he'd done was make a joke about her short hair, asking if she'd had it cut like that for a dare. She'd yelled at him; he'd pushed her; she'd pushed back; he'd pushed harder – then *smack!*

Between the trees at the edge of the clearing, which was known as the Arena, a lot of watchers still lingered. Most were younger boys who could only fantasise about being in the gang. One had a toy machine-gun; another had a plastic sword. *Short-arsed squirts!* Matt allowed himself one of the sinister smiles he'd spent hours practising in front of the mirror.

Then he saw the girl.

13

She was looking straight at him. He couldn't work out her expression, but it made him uncomfortable. He told himself that she was probably just a bit confused, but really impressed. She was very pretty with her elfin looks and long dark hair.

Matt raised a hand to wipe the sweat from his eyes, but stopped as he caught the smell. He dropped his hand, frowned and looked down. His fingers were still coated in a sticky residue of dog food. A fly buzzed near him. When he looked up again, there was an empty space where the girl had been.

An obscure sense of shame settled over him. Then he felt the rasp of Killer's tongue, and felt the dog's rubbery nose nuzzling his palm.

"Matt!" called Winston. We're going!"

Later, at home, Matt was thinking about the girl again when he realised that Mum was speaking to him. She was doing the ironing behind the settee. They'd had their tea a while ago and a smell of boiled ham and cabbage still lingered. Dad was just settling down to *The Golden Shot*. He said he watched it because Bob Monkhouse was so funny, but Mum said it was because he liked Anne Aston.

"Are you listening, Mathew?" said Mum. "I said I want you to try your blazer on. You were supposed to be coming with me this afternoon to get it."

"Yeah, okay," he said. "I'll try it on tomorrow."

"Because if it's the wrong size, I'll have to write you a note for the teachers and go up town again and change it. You should have come with me. It won't look very good, will it? If you have to go with no blazer on your first day at the Modern School."

"Stop calling it that."

"What?" she said.

"The Modern School."

"That's what it's called, ain't it? Blackthorn Mod – "

"Yeah. Blackthorn Modern School. Or just Blackthorn Modern. Not *the* Modern School. It sounds stupid."

Matt sank lower in the settee.

Dad was in his armchair, his neck and jaw dark with stubble, his Brylcreemed hair slicked back.

"It's a daft name all right," he said. "Old as the hills, that place is. Don't know how they can call it modern."

"That's not why they call it the Modern School," said Mum. "Er, why *is* it called that, Mathew?"

"Dunno," said Matt.

Dad frowned and spoke from the corner of his mouth.

"Is the kettle on?"

"I'll do it in a minute," she said, turning a shirt over and raising the iron again.

Dad sniffed and angled his head towards Matt.

"You can nip 'round the offie when *The Golden Shot*'s finished," he said.

"I'll go now. I can't stand this prat."

Dad took out a Park Drive and compressed its end by bouncing it against the face of the packet, producing a crisp assertive rap for six evenly spaced beats.

"Dot?" he said. "We got a pen and paper anywhere?"

"Sideboard drawer," said Mum. She sighed, put the iron down and made for the front room.

"Thanks, Dot," he called after her.

In its cage above the television, the budgie twirled a mirror with its beak. After each two or three goes it would stop to look at Matt, its head cocked sideways, then it would twirl the mirror again. With a mixture of boredom and contempt, he watched the budgie until Mum came back with the paper and pen.

He fetched the leather bag from the cupboard under the stairs. Then he stood waiting by the yard window. It was a sweltering hot evening and the sash window was wide open. There was a gurgle of water in next-door's kitchen drain and from somewhere else nearby in the terraced neighbourhood came the clatter-clang of a dustbin lid.

"Can I get some crisps?" he said.

Dad said nothing and scribbled his note. Smoke curled up from the ashtray on the arm of his armchair. Matt shifted the bag from one hand to the other and the empty beer bottles inside chinked together.

Then the stairs door swung open and Jenny walked in wearing a see-through top with no bra.

"Can I borrow your brolly, Mum?" she said casually. "There's supposed to be a storm later."

Matt goggled at her for a second and then kept looking into different corners of the ceiling, grinning stupidly.

"You're not going out like that!" said Mum.

"Why, what's wrong with it?"

"Just get back up to your room and get changed! Tell her, Ron!" Red in the face, Mum shot to the stairs door and held it open.

Jenny hooked her thumbs in the pockets of her flared jeans and gave Mum a rebellious glare. She'd been doing that a lot since getting back from the Isle of Wight festival last week. She'd mainly gone to see Jimi Hendrix. And, to Matt, even though Jenny was seventeen – six years older than himself – the freedom of going to something like that with her friends seemed unimaginable.

"I think it looks good, Jen," he said, glancing back.

She threw him a smile.

Dad was just cranking himself around.

"Bloody hell!" he said. "What the – Go and get some bloody clothes on!"

She stood her ground for another moment, her brown hair hanging in her face. Then she wheeled away and stomped so hard up the stairs that a sprinkle of plaster dust floated down from the ceiling. Jenny's mood made Matt feel rebellious himself. He didn't know how to express it, but thought briefly about throwing the bag of bottles across the room, or tearing the budgie squawking from its cage and dashing its head against the fireplace.

Instead, he just repeated what he'd said earlier:

"Can I get some crisps?"

It was hot again on Sunday.

With Killer bounding after the bicycles down the stony lane behind the factories, the boys headed to the vegetable allotments to help Nidge's grandad.

Soon bored with weeding, they climbed over the fence and ran off into a glaringly sunlit meadow. Killer chased rabbits. The sawing of grasshoppers was everywhere, and red admirals and cabbage whites flitted about. Hoverflies hung suspended over the heads of wild flowers.

"Wobbies," said Eddie.

"Course they're not," said Nidge. "When've you ever seen a wobbie fly like that? They're hoverflies. I've read about 'em. They're just flies, but they sort of look a bit like wasps or bees 'cause they're what you call mimics."

Nidge adjusted his glasses and gazed in turn at each of the others. His ginger hair had been recently cut into a short-back-and-sides. With a smile on his freckled face, he moved stealthily towards a hoverfly and reached out his hand. The hoverfly darted to a point a few feet away and continued hovering.

"You'll never catch one," said Eddie.

"I used to catch 'em all the time," said Nidge. "In the garden. I'd just forgot how. Watch this."

He approached another and slowly craned his hand sideways. The hoverfly hung two inches above an ox-eye daisy, its wings an almost invisible blur. Nidge's hand crept nearer, his finger and thumb poised in a C-shape that suddenly snapped shut. He held the insect under everybody's faces for inspection, pinch-gripping it by its wings. Its squirming body was striped yellow and black.

"See," he said. "Totally harmless."

17

"Clever," said Winston.

"Told you," said Nidge. He let go of the hoverfly and it disappeared across the meadow. "I used to have 'em flying on the end of a piece of cotton, tied to my finger."

"What?" said Eddie. "No chance."

"Like pets," said Nidge. "On a sort of collar or harness."

"How?" said Rick.

"Easy," said Nidge. "You just make a sort of slip-knot and hook it over the head while you're holding it by its wing, so's you've got it on a sort of lead. You have to be careful not to fasten it too tight 'round the neck. It's like a surgical operation almost – "

"No chance," said Eddie.

Since Matt's house was the nearest, he agreed to go and get a reel of cotton from his mum's sewing kit.

Within minutes of him getting back to the meadow, Nidge had a hoverfly sailing up on the end of a three-foot length of cotton. The rest began stalking the meadow with Nidge following them and offering advice. Matt managed to pinch-grip one by its wing, but it buzzed frenziedly. He felt its body vibrating against his fingertips and let it go.

"Why didn't you keep hold of it?" said Nidge.

"It buzzed. I thought it was gonna sting me."

"They're not wobbies. I told you that."

"How do you know hoverflies don't sting?"

"I just do," said Nidge. "It was in the book."

Eventually Matt held on to a hoverfly long enough to get the prepared loop over its head. It whizzed straight up and hovered at the extent of the cotton, like a tiny kite. Eddie was clumsy and impatient and had already pulled the wings off one and crushed it under his boot. Trying to help, Nidge caught another one and held it out.

"Here, Eddie," he said. "Harness 'er up!"

Matt watched with annoyance as Eddie made a crude loop in his cotton, slipped it vaguely over the hoverfly's head and pulled on the ends.

"Oh, crap," said Nidge. "He's decapitated the bleeder."

A smirk spread across Eddie's face.

An hour later, the boys had two hooked up each, and went back to the allotment to show Nidge's grandad.

"I ain't never seen nowt like it," said the bent old man from under his flat cap. "Ruddy barmy, you lot."

Throughout the morning, word spread and other boys and a few girls joined in. Killer bounded and howled crazily, chasing anything that moved.

Everybody tumbled about the hot meadow among the long grass, cornflowers, ox-eye daisies and poppies.

By lunchtime, sixteen of them were crowding around Nidge's bemused grandad on the allotment, pet hoverflies swarming overhead in their dozens.

Matt and Nidge went to the park later and spotted Jenny and her friends sitting on the grass. There were about ten of them in a circle, smoking and passing bottles of wine around. They were still talking about the music festival.

One guy with really long hair and a flowery shirt was lying back smiling up at the blue sky.

"So-ooo groovy!" he said. "Isle of Wight, 1970. Europe's answer to Woodstock."

Jenny was wearing her see-through top. She had a cardigan beside her on the grass. The man she seemed to be with picked up a guitar and asked what music the boys liked, then laughed when Nidge said Deep Purple. But he did a reasonable job of 'Black Night'.

Matt kept looking around the park, hoping that the pretty girl he'd seen in the woods yesterday might show up, but she never did.

4

Off-Side

From Vonnie's bedroom window, she could see for miles.

At the back of the semi-detached houses, the gardens were long; then there was a stretch of scrubby wasteland known as the Twicken. Beyond the Twicken, the green canopy of Blackthorn Woods rolled out to countryside in the north and the east. Between the housing estate and the town, the woods were narrower, offering short-cuts to the other housing estates, the main road and the shops.

Trying not to think too much about the new school-blazer and skirt hanging on the back of the door, she sat on the edge of her bed with her book.

... Agata spent long hours with the hammers and chisels, trying to fashion stone, trying to master the skills her father had taken great pains to show her.

When he could no longer pretend that she was a boy, he lost interest in her. He drank more mead and was often cross without reason.

"I'm sorry, daughter," he said eventually. "Your path is different. I don't know what your path is, but it's not the path of stone."

One day, he gave a painted wooden sign to Agata to wear around her neck. The sign said, KICK ME. *And from that day onwards, wherever she went, people kicked her. Market traders came out from their stalls, grinning as they kicked her backside. Boys who used to be her friends, read the words on the sign, laughed*

and swung their boots. Even a kindly old fishwife
kicked Agata, apologising as she did so ...

Another argument had started downstairs and it was
affecting Vonnie's concentration. *Argument?* Arguments
were usually between at least two people, weren't they?
When Skinner and Mam argued, it was more like a
torrent of hard words and spite from him, and apologies
and occasional, appeasing soft words from her. Skinner
could keep going for hours when it was this bad, and
then it often ended with a slamming of doors and with
Skinner setting about some job or other on his car.

She went to the window again and looked out across
Blackthorn Woods. Although out of sight, on lower
ground in the middle distance to the east, Vonnie knew the
exact place where the railway line curved around Gallows
Hill. In her mind, she pictured a freight train slowing for
the bend around the hill.

It was worse than Matt could have imagined.

Straight after the tinned-salmon sandwiches for Sunday
tea, Mum had sent him to his room to try the uniform on.
The blazer was a stupid bottle-green colour. The tie was
the same but with yellow stripes. The grey trousers were
sharply creased down the legs. And the shoes were shiny
black things with long square toes and a brogue pattern;
they squeaked when he walked.

Yesterday morning, at the barber's shop with Rick,
Matt's mousey hair had been cropped into a short-back-
and-sides. It had seemed all right then. But now, as he
examined himself in the wardrobe mirror, he was shocked
at how much the haircut made his face look wedge-
shaped, emphasising how square and tapering his chin
was ... Just like the new shoes!

His old Wayfinders were on the floor in the corner. It
was hard to think about never wearing them again. There

was a compass in one of the heels and originally there'd been different kinds of animal prints on the soles. Now they were too small and letting water.

Matt squeaked over to the window.

As he stood there, he heard the front door opening, and looked down in time to see Mum putting the empty milk bottles on the doorstep before ducking back inside.

In a dismal kind of way, Matt was comforted by the familiarity of Grebble Street's terraced houses. He decided that he liked the brick chimneys, the H-shaped TV aerials and the blue slate roofs.

Then an image of Blackthorn Modern sprang into his head – a grim, featureless sprawl of buildings behind grey iron railings. Through its windows, he'd often seen the uniformed hordes washing like a faceless tide along the upper and lower corridors.

He thought about his friends. And about how they'd now be scattered in different form classes and subject groups. All he wanted was to build a shack in the woods with the gang and never go to school again.

Before Matt knew it, a month had passed. His most hated period in the timetable was P.E. Or Games, as it was called. It was compulsory, twice a week. To begin with, the focus of the Games periods for his group had been gymnastics and the running track.

On the Tuesday afternoon in the middle of October, Mr Hurst promised to take them onto the playing fields for their first football session. Matt was having a bad enough day already. On his way to the gym, he was ambushed on "the bridge" by some second-formers.

Greenie's gang were feared throughout the school, even feared by many third-formers.

"Got any rocks?" said Greenie, a short, chubby boy with a red-around-the-eyes, tired look.

"Rocks?" said Matt.

"Sweets, you prat."

"No," said Matt, backing off. "I've not."

Almost everybody else had gone to their lessons, so he was alone on the bridge with Greenie, Sturgess, and the big stupid one they called "the Gonk".

The bridge was a recent construction that spanned between two of the school buildings at first-floor level. It was closed in, with a curved tin roof and Perspex windows for its full length. Spread out below were the shrubs and pathways of the outdoor foyer area.

"Every rock on you," said Sturgess. He was tall and mean-looking, and had a reputation for random violence.

Matt was made to raise his arms while Sturgess went through every pocket.

"What's this then?" he said, pulling out a crumpled, dirty paper-bag with congealed Pear Drops and blazer fluff stuck in the bottom. "Ee-yurr! You can keep 'em."

But the Gonk snatched the sticky mess from Sturgess, de-bagged and de-fluffed the Pear Drops, and put them in his mouth happily. The Gonk had a wild shock of dark hair, a rugged, pimply face, and was a head taller than any other boys in the second form.

Greenie and Sturgess laughed.

"Eat anything, the Gonk will," said Sturgess.

Matt had been backed up to the handrail with his head against the windows. Now, Greenie looked him over with a leisurely air, as if wondering what additional sport might be had. He leaned forward and kissed Matt on the cheek.

"Just make sure you've got some decent rocks for us the next time we see you," he said.

Then he led the other two away and Matt went in the opposite direction across the bridge.

By the time he reached the gym and the changing rooms, he had to hurry to get ready.

It was raining steadily when Mr Hurst, the strictest of the Games teachers, led Matt's afternoon group out to the playing fields. Matt was slightly shocked that the football was still going ahead in the rain. He'd thought, as well, that Mr Hurst would probably be explaining the rules. He didn't. There was an assumption that all boys knew how to play football, so they were going to get on with playing a game straight away.

Matt had never followed or been interested in football. The excitement that so many boys gushed over it was a mystery to him. Marty Hollis was one such boy. He knew the game inside out.

"Are we playing off-sides, sir?" he asked.

"No," Mr Hurst replied.

"Sir? Can I be centre forward on my team, sir?"

"We'll see."

"Sir? Sir? How do you think City'll do against Wolves on Saturday, sir?"

And so on.

Teams and positions were decided by Mr Hurst, a coin was flipped, a whistle blown, and it was "kick off". Ten minutes later, Matt was hugging himself against the wind and rain as he paced the shallow basin of muddy water between the goal posts. The ball had been up the other end of the pitch so far, with Mr Hurst supervising a succession of corners, free kicks and throw-ins.

Suddenly Marty Hollis was tearing down the wing and the defenders of Matt's team were nowhere in sight. Matt's football boots made squelching sounds as he shuffled from side to side trying to cover the goal mouth.

Marty was closing fast, and about to take a shot that was sure to find its mark and leave Matt eating mud. Before that could happen, Marty's legs slid from under him and he landed flat on his back.

The ball continued rolling straight towards Matt. It had almost stopped when he picked it up, but he felt a glow of pride. He'd saved it! He glanced about the pitch, smiling and half expecting a cheer. Nobody seemed interested.

The defenders had fallen back to mark the rest of the attack squad. A couple of opposition players crowded in on Matt, shouting and jutting their hands in the air. Mr Hurst had moved up the pitch, too, but he was observing the action from ten yards away.

"They're blocking me, sir," said Matt.

"Do something then, Baxter!"

Marty started swinging his boot at the ball, a couple of times nearly dislodging it from Matt's grip.

"He's kicking it, sir," said Matt. "He can't kick it while I'm holding it, can he?"

"He can do anything he likes to try to get the ball, as long as he doesn't use his hands. Come on, Baxter! Kick it to somebody!"

Matt dodged sideways, then – with the idea of taking a run-up and kicking the ball out as far as he could – he took three steps backwards.

Marty laughed and grabbed his nearest team mate in a brief hug. Both boys skipped in circles around the penalty area, jumping up and down and shouting, "Goal! goal! goal! goal!"

Matt looked at Mr Hurst. But Mr Hurst only shook his head and smiled in a bitter-sweet way, then turned to the rest of the players.

"One–nil!" he announced.

"What's happening?" said Matt.

"You stepped back into the goal," said Mr Hurst.

"But I was going to take a run-up, sir. They were in the way. They kept blocking me. I – "

"You stepped over the line with the ball. You're still standing inside the goal now, holding the ball. It's a goal."

At Matt's feet, all he could see was mud and water, but he was standing well behind any straight line that might have been drawn between the goal posts.

"I'm the goalie though, sir. Can't I – "

"The ball went over the line."

"But – "

"It makes no difference if you're the goalie."

"Oh," said Matt. "Is that what you call an off-side, then?"

Mr Hurst gave him a strange, pitying look.

"Can someone else go in goal, sir?"

"No, Baxter. You're staying in for the rest of this game. Just don't do anything half-witted like that again." He jogged up the pitch, blowing a series of short peeps on his whistle. "Right, everybody! Get in position for a centre."

The play became concentrated at the other end for a while. Matt wished he could be with the main pack, more anonymous. Maybe he would even be lucky enough to score. He imagined himself getting carried back to the changing-rooms on the friendly shoulders of his cheering team-mates. Matt Baxter. Striker. Hero of the match.

As it turned out, his team scored an equaliser in the second half, then the opposition scored two goals in the final fifteen minutes. The first was a flying header from Marty, which stung Matt's fingertips as he dived for it. The second was a long shot from one of their defenders, which came out of nowhere as Matt was leaning against a goal post with his hands down the front of his shorts.

Back in the changing-rooms, some of the boys' faces were filled with hatred and others with smug mockery.

"What are you?" said Brian Smith, lashing his wet kit across Matt's bare back. "Stoopid ... stoopid ... stoopid ... stoopid ..." He lashed out again with each word.

Other boys laughed. Spiteful grins and shining eyes took pleasure in Matt's misery. The air stank of sweat and feet. Brian lashed out again and Matt spun abruptly and aimed a punch. The blow didn't connect, but Brian staggered back with a surprised expression.

Then Mr Hurst emerged naked from his little office.

"Get showered, lads. Smith? Baxter? What's going on?"

"Nothing, sir."

"Nothing, sir."

Everybody continued taking their kit off. Some of the braver boys joined Mr Hurst in the communal shower, but most waited until he'd finished and gone back into his little office-cum-changing-room.

Water needled from the pitted chrome showerheads or came out in fat curving jets where the fittings were missing. The floor was bare concrete. The wall tiles were the colour of neglected teeth.

Matt washed himself hurriedly, taking what privacy he could in the billowing steam. The antagonism towards him seemed to be waning as it was replaced by bawdy jokes. There were no inhibitions as genitals were scrutinised, judged and commented on.

"Call that a willy, Cartwright?" said Steve Cooper.

Matt's penis was nothing to brag about, but standing there among the jumbled bodies, he was comforted by realising that he was of average size.

He pointed at Cartwright and joined the laughter.

5

Blackthorn Modern

... Agata tried removing the sign. Within moments, a deep swoon came over her, and she awoke to find the sign back around her neck. She tried burning it, but a swoon came over her and she awoke to find it, as new, back around her neck. Agata puzzled over her allotted role. She wanted to talk to her father about it, but he was never in a talking mood these days.

He drank more and more mead and had no time for Agata's questions. One night, while staggering home from the tavern, he fell into a horses' water-trough. He drowned and was buried the next afternoon.

Nobody attended the funeral except Agata. A man of the cloth read some lines from a book, then closed the book reverentially and proceeded to give Agata a good kicking. Agata was grateful that restraint had been shown until the service was over. The grave diggers, who'd just lowered the coffin, kicked Agata as well. They kicked her so hard that she fell into the grave. Then they were angry with her for holding up their work of filling in the hole, so they pulled her out and kicked her all the way to the gates of the churchyard, and sent her off into the rain ...

A bus ran from the top of Vonnie's road that could drop her directly outside school, but the buses were horribly smoky. It was bad enough with Skinner's fags in the house. She could have cycled, too, but she didn't like some of the morons who hung about in the bike sheds. So, like most other mornings during the five weeks or so that she'd been at Blackthorn Modern, she set off on foot.

"You can get it if you really want ..." sang Desmond Dekker on the kitchen radio, and Vonnie would have stayed to listen, but she was running late.

She left the house by the kitchen door and squeezed between the brick wall and Skinner's metallic-bronze Ford Zodiac. Then it was down the path, passing the garage and shed on her left, the lawn and rockery on her right. The rockery had lots of alpine plants and four concrete gnomes. These gnomes were something that Skinner took pride in. Every couple of years, when the paintwork was starting to fade and flake, he'd take them into the garage, sand them until they were bare and pale grey, then spend his spare time for several weeks hand-painting them before returning them to the rockery.

Vonnie hated Skinner's gnomes.

It was a long garden that ended with a broken-down chicken-wire fence that could easily be stepped over. The hundred-yard expanse of grassy, scrubby wasteland – the Twicken – gave directly onto Blackthorn Woods.

The air in the woods was pungent this morning, filled with the smells of loamy soil and abundant ferns. The ground was soft and crumbly, and dappled with light and shade from the sunshine through the canopy.

A pair of swifts darted across Vonnie's path.

The sight of the two birds made her think again about the mystery of maleness and femaleness.

What is it to be a girl? What is it to be a boy?

She didn't mean the physical differences. Or anything to do with a man's or woman's role in creating babies. She didn't really know for certain what she meant. But she'd never understood the whole pram-and-doll thing that appealed to most girls from the youngest age upwards.

Blackthorn Modern had been a reminder that she was different. She'd tried to be friendly with a few girls in her form class, but found that she simply didn't care about the same music, comics or hobbies. Vonnie wasn't sure what she did care about. It seemed to her that a lot of her time and energy went into avoiding trouble at home.

When she arrived in the school playground, Nidge, Eddie, Matt, Winston and Rick were in their usual spot near the dinner-hall windows. Matt was rolling a large conker in the palm of his hand, and marvelling at the way the autumn sunlight fell on its reddish-brown surface.

"Look how it shines," he said.

"Not much use shining, is it?" said Eddie. "You've been carrying it about in your pocket all week."

"It's a big 'un," said Rick. "You'll beat anybody. Give Badger a go when you see him; he had one yesterday."

Matt held the conker up for everyone to see. He smiled as it dangled from its clean white plimsoll lace.

None of this made much sense to Vonnie. But it made more sense than hopscotch, Sindy dolls or nurses' outfits – although Mam was a nurse so maybe that wasn't very fair. Vonnie didn't consider any of the boys as friends exactly, but she tended to hang about somewhere near their gatherings at break times.

"Hi, Vonnie," said Matt. "What do you think of it?"

"Yeah, it's a good conker," she said.

"I spent ages making the hole," he said. "Borrowed one of the old man's drills and just kept twisting it in."

"What, by hand?" said Nidge.

"Yeah, well I wanted to do it really careful."

"Where's yours?" said Eddie, addressing Vonnie. "You gonna challenge him?"

"Why would you think I've got one?" she said.

"Dunno," he said, flicking his gaze over her short hair. "I just thought you might of."

"No," she said, looking at him steadily.

Eddie laughed and turned away.

"Conkers are for kids anyway," he said.

Matt's cheeks flushed and Vonnie saw him tuck the conker into his blazer pocket. A moment later, conkers were the last thing on anybody's mind.

"You! Yeah, you! Get here!"

It was Sturgess – one of Greenie's gang.

Nobody with any sense messed with Greenie's gang.

Vonnie saw that the "you" Sturgess was singling out with his finger was Nidge.

"What?" said Nidge calmly. "What do you want?"

"I said get here!"

"Get lost."

Sturgess strode over, grabbed Nidge and thrust him up against the wall. Nidge made choking sounds as he tried to prise apart the fists joined under his chin. His head was wedged between the drainpipe and the brickwork, and only the toes of his shoes were touching the ground.

Nidge's friends should be helping, thought Vonnie. If they tried to help, she probably would. But she wasn't going to make the first move. Was she? She looked around at the others – Matt, Winston, Eddie, Rick – and saw her own outraged helplessness reflected back at her.

"I've heard all about you lot," Sturgess spat into Nidge's face. "You go in the woods together and fiddle about with each other's bums, don't you?"

Nidge's glasses hung lopsided. He clawed at Sturgess's fists and made gurgling noises as he tried to speak.

"*Don't you?*" said Sturgess.

"No," managed Nidge.

Vonnie moved forward, then stopped. They should be doing something; they should be punching, kicking, hair-pulling – anything.

Then it was over. Nidge had been released. He slid down the wall and folded easily onto the ground.

Sturgess considered the rest of them.

"First-form sprogs!" he said before swaggering off.

31

He joined Greenie, the Gonk and a few others who'd been watching from across the playground.

Nidge got up and stumbled about in the indentation of the drain, looking like a new-born foal, or as if he'd forgotten how to walk. Vonnie felt ashamed that she hadn't helped. She picked Nidge's fountain pen up from the tarmac and handed it to him. He thanked her absently. His hands shook as he straightened his glasses; his freckled face had broken out in red blotches.

None of the boys could make eye-contact with Nidge. Rick kept striking his foot across the ground and making sparks fly from the metal Blakeys embedded in his shoes. There were some relieved laughs and feeble comments on the fascinating subject of Blakeys. Then Nidge spat in the direction Sturgess had gone, and that seemed to close the matter, because – although Nidge was still pressing his fingers delicately about his throat – he said in a deadpan way, "What've you got first period, Matt?"

"French, worst luck," said Matt.

And Vonnie understood that this was partly what it meant to be a boy at Blackthorn Modern. You had to put on a brave face at times like this.

"I thought he was really going to *do* you," said one of three girls who'd arrived on the scene.

It was Dawn Hagley, a girl with long dark hair who was in Vonnie's form class. Vonnie noticed that Matt was smiling goofily at Dawn.

"Your mates didn't do much to help," said one of the other girls.

"Nothing they *could* have done," said Nidge. "Sturgess is rock-hard."

"He smacked both the Mason brothers up in the quad last week," gushed Dawn. "There was blood everywhere. It was a great laugh!"

A great laugh? thought Vonnie.

"What do you think *you're* gawping at?" said Dawn.

Vonnie blinked, but then realised that Dawn's words were aimed at Matt.

"Not you for a start," said Matt, but he looked as if he instantly regretted the comment.

The bell clanged out and everybody began dawdling across the playground.

Spotting Badger leaning outside the entrance with a miserable face, Eddie lurched ahead and delivered a savage blow to the boy's arm. In surprise, Badger dropped the plimsolls and tee-shirt he'd been holding. He stooped down and picked them up.

"Where've you been?" said Eddie.

"I've was trying to borrow some kit," said Badger. "I've got plimmies and a shirt but no shorts. Can anyone lend me any? Thommo makes you do gym in your pants if you ain't got no shorts."

"Is that conker of yours still going?" said Eddie. "You've got a challenger. Come on, Matt. Not frit, are you?"

"No, not frit," said Matt, a flush on his cheeks. "It's just that ... there's not enough time."

"Course there is," said Eddie. "You've only got Griffiths next. She's as soft as kitten kak."

Vonnie remembered Eddie's earlier comment, and she thought that Matt had probably convinced himself by now that conkers was a game for small children. It didn't help that Dawn and her friends were crowding in to watch, whispering and giggling among themselves.

Badger took a conker from his blazer pocket and held it out on its frayed string. It was barely half the size of Matt's and had a flat face on one side.

"Cheeser," said Winston.

Matt wound the end of the plimsoll lace round his index and middle fingers. He took aim, lunged and missed. The second shot was a hit and the third another miss.

Badger's three shots were all on target, and the last produced a loud *thunk!* Matt inspected his conker and

33

looked shocked. Vonnie could see a crack stretching from top to bottom of the reddish-brown surface. By the time Matt had taken his second-round shots, the crack had widened, exposing the nutty yellow interior.

Badger took aim again. On his first shot, the strings snagged. The second shot left Matt holding an empty lace.

"Soz, Matt," said Badger. "I'll give you mine if you like."

Matt shook his head and turned for the entrance.

"It's only a conker," said Dawn. "He looks as if he's about to cry!"

6

Vampire Lovers

Matt was standing outside the Ritzy cinema on Main Street when Vonnie pulled up on the pavement, the brakes of her drop-handlebar racer squealing briefly. She leaned the racer against the wall and stood beside him to look at the poster advertising the latest film. Matt's bike had been out of action all year, and he was on his way to the six o'clock gang meeting on foot.

"You'd never get in to see that," said Vonnie. "Not even with an adult. It's an 'X' film."

"Hi, Vonnie. Yeah, I know. It looks brilliant though."

The glazed doors of the Art Deco building were closed and unlit, the cinema not yet open for the evening showing of *The Vampire Lovers*. The colourful poster showed scantily clad people chained to a wall. There were flaming torches and a skull, and a group of women – presumably the vampires – with long dark hair, heavy make-up, and long flowing low-cut dresses. Their arms were raised and their fingers contorted claw-like. Matt imagined himself as one of the men chained to the wall, and Dawn as one of the vampire women, laughing and saying: "It's only a conker. He looks as if he's about to cry!"

"ENTER IF YOU DARE ..." the poster declared, "taste the deadly passion of the BLOOD-NYMPHS!"

"Ingrid Pitt, George Cole, Kate O'Mara, Peter Cushing," Matt read. "Peter Cushing's always in the best horror films. There was this really amazing-looking one last year called *Frankenstein Must Be Destroyed*".

"That sounds a bit stupid," said Vonnie.

"What? No – "

"I wouldn't mind seeing *The Vampire Lovers*. What are you up to anyway?"

"Gang meeting. What about you?"

"Just riding around. Where's the gang meeting?"

"In the woods. HQ. We've got seats and that."

"Great," said Vonnie.

"Yeah, we've got loads of different dens in the woods. I've got my own secret den as well, and I'm in the middle of building a shack."

"Groovy."

"Yeah," said Matt, although he hadn't started on it, or even found a place for it yet. "I hate school, and when the shack's ready I'm going to live in it and never go back."

Vonnie stared at him.

"Sounds a bit like a story I read. You could probably find things like berries and roots to eat in the woods."

"That's exactly what I was planning," said Matt. "And I'll have a camping stove set up to cook stuff."

"Long as you know what stuff's poisonous though," she said. "I'm leaving home as well soon. I might just jump on a freight train and see where it takes me. Or maybe I could stay in your shack some nights when it's finished."

"Ready in two weeks," said Matt with conviction. "You'd have to bring your own blankets. Anyway, I'd better get going. I'm late for the meeting."

"Right," said Vonnie. "I'll give you a croggy to the end of Horsefair Road if you like."

"What? Really? Yeah ..."

Vonnie pulled her bike away from the wall and straddled the cross-bar, one foot on a pedal, leaving the saddle free for Matt. She was wearing training shoes, jeans and a denim jacket over a purple tee-shirt. Matt was wearing trainers and jeans as well, and a brown corduroy jacket of the type Nidge seemed to favour. He climbed onto the bike awkwardly and Vonnie set off, surprising him by giving as good a croggy as any boy.

"I suppose you could come to the gang meeting," he said. "If you wanted to ..."

Vonnie said nothing.

"Mind you," he added. "I don't know what Nidge might say. Or the others."

"It's okay," said Vonnie. "Just let me know when the shack's finished."

Various forms of seating had found their way to HQ. There was the old car-seat that Nidge always sat in – the same car-seat he'd had boys carrying him around in back in the summer; it had been scavenged from an old Austin Cambridge abandoned at the edge of the woods on Shady Lane. Matt had a wooden dining-chair with its legs missing. Eddie had a shabby grey-and-red leather pouffe. The others were more or less left to squabble for next best places among the remaining boxes and milk crates that completed a rough horseshoe arrangement.

"... so we stick together at school as much as possible," Nidge was saying as Matt arrived. "Safety in numbers."

"Soz I'm late," said Matt.

"Anyway," said Nidge. "I'm not talking about Sturgess no more. We'll get him back one day. Right ... so ... Don't forget sub-money. Some of you still haven't paid last week's yet. It's only tuppence a week. Just give it to me or Matt. Right ... so ... Anyone else got any business?"

"Got sent to Deakin this afto," said Sammy, a thin boy still wearing his school trousers and a brown anorak. "If I cheek Miss Soames again, Deakin's giving me the whack."

"Size 12 plimmy," said Eddie, who'd already had the whack for skiving out of a maths period.

"They're all gits," said Winston. "Deakin, the teachers, Sturgess, and all of Greenie's gang – "

"We'll get 'em all back one day," said Nidge.

There were general murmurs of assent.

"I saw that Vonnie girl on the way here," said Matt. "She gave me a croggy. She seems okay. Bit of a laugh. Nearly brought her to the meeting."

"What?" said Nidge. "No girls allowed."

"No. I know. Anyway there's this new film on at the flicks about vampires."

"My brother and his mates seen it last night," said Badger. "They're all about seventeen or eighteen. If a vampire bites you, right, you turn into one. But they're frit of crosses and holy water and onions – "

"Garlic," said Matt.

"Yeah. Or garlic. And there's this bit in it, right, where this bloke has to kill a vampire, but it's really hard to kill 'em, and they sleep in coffins and everything – but this bloke, right, he finds one of the vampires asleep in a coffin and he rams this wooden stake straight through its heart."

"Sounds fantastic," said Matt.

"Yeah, my brother reckons it was."

"Vampires don't really exist though," said Rick.

"They do," said Badger. "They live in massive castles. And sometimes in woods and forests and stuff."

He sniffed, wiped his runny nose on his sleeve and looked wide-eyed towards the dusky spaces between the trees at the edge of the clearing.

"They're not real," said Rick.

"Maybe not in England," said Badger. "It's where they've got these massive castles. France or Italy or somewhere."

"If there's any vampires still alive," said Nidge. "It'll be in the Carpathian Mountains in Romania. I read about it."

"Yeah, that's what I meant," said Badger. "France or Romania. Somewhere like that. I think my brother might of been there last year ... and might of even saw one ..."

Nidge adjusted his glasses on his nose. He flinched at the sound of twigs cracking nearby.

"What's that?" said Sammy.

"It's nothing," said Nidge, surveying the trees.

A breeze blew dust about the clearing.

"There's no vampires in England," said Nidge. "Or in these woods. But it's getting a bit dark now ... so the meeting's sort of over."

Three hours later, Matt was half in the living-room and half out, sitting on the bottom corner of the stairs with the stairs door open. His buttocks were numb and he could feel a draught on the back of his neck that blew down the narrow closed-in stair passage from an unknown source.

The settee had been shoved up near the television and the table had been pulled out from the wall – the usual arrangement for Dad's turn at hosting card night. Fag smoke trickled up and hung against the ceiling.

"Your call, Walshie," said Dad. "Gone sleep again?"

There was laughter from the other men.

Dad took a swallow of beer and leaned back, his belly white and hairy in the spaces where his shirt strained open between the buttons.

"Sorry, Ron," said Walshie. "I'll raise it to half-a-crown."

"Can't raise a blind man," said Frank. "I'm still blind, and the bet's two bob, but only a bob for me until I open."

"Sorry. Two bob then."

"And two bob," said Frank, pushing coins in.

"And two," said Dad.

Matt loved how the rhythms of the game rose and fell, the clatter and chime of coins, the guarded glimpses at hands. But he could hardly believe the old-fashioned words they still used for money. A "bob" was a shilling, or five new pence. And "half-a-crown" was twelve-and-a-half new pence. The 5p, 10p and 50p coins were already in circulation, ahead of full decimalisation in February next year. Parents and old people didn't understand. There was even a stupid song by Max Bygraves to help them.

"Another bob blind," said Frank.

What Matt did like was the special language of the card game. *Can't raise a blind man*, he said in his mind. *Ace high*. Or *queen flush*. And *stacking*. *Stacking* was one of his favourites. It was a decision that always seemed to be made with difficulty and maybe a wistful glance at the money in the pot that had been risked and then lost.

The betting continued, the men tossing coins in the middle in a mechanical blasé process. The stake was five shillings when Frank swore and skimmed his three cards face-down across the table. Walshie stacked next, then Sid.

"Just me and thee again, Ron," said Archie. "I'll raise it to ten shillings."

It was months since Matt had seen a bet as high as ten shillings. That made the pot more than five pounds, maybe not far off ten. Matt marvelled as he calculated how many cinema tickets it could buy, how many bottles of Tizer.

Dad drank some beer and looked about. He'd winked at Matt not long ago; now he seemed annoyed.

"You still up?" he said. "Nip in the kitchen and ask your mother if the sandwiches are ready."

Matt got up from the bottom corner of the stairs and crossed the room, catching sight of Archie's cards on the way – a jack, a queen and a king, all of them diamonds.

He lingered in the kitchen doorway and watched as Dad took a ten-shilling note from his wallet and put it in the pot. Without hesitation, Archie slid a 50p piece forward. Dad frowned suspiciously, although he would have known that the coin had the same value, and that ten-shilling notes were going out of circulation in a month's time.

He became pensive and reached for his cigarettes, slid one out and rapped it six times against the packet. The rapping was followed by the dull flutter of the budgie's wings on the cage bars.

"Go on," said Dad. "Go and ask your mother about the sandwiches. And stay in there now."

Matt slipped into the kitchen.

"Haven't you gone to bed yet, Mathew?"

The washing machine juddered violently on the faded lino. Mum was sitting at the small drop-leaf table reading a paperback, and an empty mug stood in front of her on the Formica top.

"Not tired," he said, sitting on one of the high stools with the blue Fablon peeling off. "Can I have a sarnie?"

"I suppose so. Luncheon meat or cheese? Or I've got a nice bit of haslet?"

"Haslet and pickle."

As she went to the pantry, Matt looked at the cover of her book. It showed a tanned and muscular man on the deck of a luxury yacht. A blonde woman was smiling up at him from the walkway of a marina.

Mum set a loaf of bread on the table and took some things from the fridge.

"Where's Jenny tonight?" said Matt.

"Oh, a few of her friends took her to the pub to try and cheer her up. You know how upset she's been about that Jimi Hendrix chap dying last month."

"Yeah. I know. He was an amazing guitarist."

"Tragic," said Mum. "So young."

Matt threw himself back on the stool and it pivoted up on two legs. There was the delicious stomach-churning moment as the stool tilted beyond the point of balance, then his shoulders made contact with the wall and he was wedged there, smiling.

"Them legs'll slide out one of these days," said Mum.

"No they won't," said Matt. "Dad told me to ask if their sandwiches are ready."

She laid out ten slices of bread and began buttering them. The washing machine made a low whining sound.

Matt dropped forward and down off the stool, and went to the side window. Because of the dog-leg layout of the house, it was possible to see diagonally across the yard to the living-room window, but Matt was disappointed. The curtain had been drawn. He went to the half-open living-room door instead and peered around.

"Here," said Mum. "Your sandwich is nearly ready."

Matt tried to make out what was going on with the card game. From where he stood, all he could see was a corner of the dining table, somebody's tattooed arm and part of Frank's bearded face. But he could hear everything.

Archie had put a pound in the pot to "see" Dad's hand. A moment later, there was a low whistle.

"A run," said Frank. "Four-five-six. Nice one, Ron."

There was another pause.

Then Archie said, "Sorry, Ronnie boy. Not good enough. Jack-queen-king. On the bounce."

On the bounce. Matt knew that expression, too.

If you had something on the bounce, it was brilliant. You kept on betting no matter what. A picture of the jack, queen and king of diamonds he'd seen on his way to the kitchen glowed brightly in his mind.

He imagined himself travelling around Europe with Dawn when they were ten years older, maybe cruising about the Mediterranean on a luxury yacht. He'd be filthy rich, sailing into tropical sunsets with Dawn by his side in a bikini. They'd live forever – because they'd be vampires with their coffins hidden in a castle in Romania. Matt's hobby would be playing cards in the big casinos of Monte Carlo or somewhere. Dawn would be next to him in a low-cut dress as he sat around a green-baize table at the biggest game in town. And he'd lay down his hand to the goggle-eyed reaction of the other players.

Soz, everybody. Jack-queen-king. On the bounce.

7

Cordon Bleu

"What I can't understand, for the life of me," said Skinner, grinning hugely, "is how anybody manages to get a steak-and-kidney pie burnt on the outside and stone-cold raw on the inside. I didn't even know it was possible."

Vonnie laughed. She wasn't comfortable with laughing at Mam's cooking, but because the atmosphere in the house was so miserable most of the time, it was hard not be swept along when Skinner was in a good mood.

It had been an okay Monday at school, too – the first day back following autumn half-term. The highlight of the week's holiday had been the Ritzy's showing of *When Dinosaurs Ruled The Earth*. Vonnie had been to see it once with Matt and the others, but she knew that the boys had been three times altogether. Everybody had talked about the film at school all day. And then Vonnie had chatted with Matt about the shack again this afternoon because they were in the same geography group.

At Skinner's remark, Mam had stood up.

"I could pop it back in the oven for a bit," she said.

'That's no good," said Skinner. "The crust'll get burnt even more. I like to see a nice golden-brown crust on my steak-and-kidney pie."

"Well, perhaps I could scrape the filling out and – "

"No. Sit down. Leave it."

Vonnie laughed again and said, "I prefer the crust burnt and the filling cold."

Skinner gazed steadily at her.

"You're a silly sod," he said.

43

Vonnie made a loony face, enjoying the attention and colluding to look even more of a "silly sod". These rare moments of repartee with Skinner – strictly on *his* terms, of course – were like taking a big bite from a cream cake and finding dirt in the middle, but the cake was so nice that you carried on eating it along with the dirt. She jabbed her fork into her steak-and-kidney pie and was pleased to see that it stayed upright like a flagpole when she let go.

Mam made a funny, warbling, exasperated sigh that sounded as if she were trying to yodel.

"I don't know!" she said, smiling. "Work my fingers to the bone to please you lot, and look at the thanks I get. You should watch yourselves. Or you never know what I might put inside the next pie."

She picked up her packet of mentholated cigarettes, paused, then tossed them over her shoulder and helped herself cheekily to Skinner's Benson & Hedges.

Skinner grinned appreciatively.

"You're a one, you are," he said. "My funny old ..."

Vonnie looked up, thinking for a moment that he was about to use Mam's name, Brenda.

"Yeah ... you're a one, you are," he concluded.

He pushed his plate away, leaned back in his chair and clasped his hands behind his head.

"Well I don't think you'll be offered a job at Berni Inns in the near future. You'd better stick to nursing."

Mam laughed. She poured milk into three mugs and lifted the knitted tea-cosy off the teapot.

"Mind you," said Skinner. "Could have been a top chef myself, if I'd wanted. Always had a knack for throwing a square meal together."

"Like when Mam fell over in the bathroom last year," said Vonnie, "and she was all bruised up and couldn't get out of bed all over Christmas and you did the cooking."

Mam paused in the middle of pouring the tea. Skinner spotted something very distracting in a corner of the ceiling, and Vonnie followed his gaze, expecting to see a big spider, but there was nothing there.

"What?" she said. "What is it?"

She'd only been trying to keep the jokey mood going, and she couldn't understand their reactions.

"Yeah, and *you* did the cooking …" she said to Skinner.

Skinner brightened.

"I did, didn't I?" he said. "Running up and down and all over the house, I was. Breakfasts, dinners, teas."

"Yeah," said Vonnie, "yeah! And the Christmas dinner was mental. The spuds still had peel left on."

"That's right!" he said. "But that was your job, peeling the spuds. And the gravy you made was all lumpy."

Without looking away from Vonnie, he automatically took the mug of tea Mam held out for him.

"I know!" said Vonnie. "But you were the main chef. And that old washing-up bowl you dragged out from under the sink to wash the vegetables in – that wasn't supposed to be used for anything like that. A few years before, I had a verruca from the swimming baths, and I used to use that bowl to wash my foot in every night before I put the stuff on the doctor gave me."

Skinner howled with laughter.

"We've probably all of us got verrucas growing in our stomachs," he said.

"If I remember that meal rightly," said Mam. "I found the big chunky stem from the cabbage on my plate."

"Yeah, that should have gone in the bin," said Skinner.

"So should the potato peel," said Vonnie. "And that scrawny little turkey was almost cremated!"

Skinner slapped the table; his eyes were shining with tears of laughter.

"I can just picture it now. Your mam with cindered turkey, verruca vegetables, lumpy gravy and the heel of the cabbage! Mind you, it was still a square meal."

Mam shook her head.

"I don't know. You two." She gripped the edge of the table and began to stand. "You ready for pudding, Bill?"

"What is it?"

"Angel Delight."

"Yeah, that sounds okay," he said.

He nudged his dinner plate with the side of his hand.

"And do me a favour and get the rest of this muck out from under my nose, will you? There's a love."

... The next morning, Agata packed a knapsack and travelled away from that town of bad people. She determined to live somewhere else and find work. But wherever she went, whoever she approached, people read what was on the sign and kicked her.

She knew that the words were the problem. So she travelled the land searching for someone who might know how to help. When people weren't busy kicking her, they listened to her question, then shook their heads. "Yes," they all agreed, "the words are the problem." But nobody could help.

Every night, she ate roots and berries by her nomad's fire, then slept under the great mystery of the whirling cosmos. At dawn, she rubbed her face with ashes from the dead fire and went on her way.

She searched for many years, until one day she heard about a cranky old mystic who lived at the top of a mountain. It was a three-day climb. On the third day, Agata was almost blown off the mountain by a snowstorm, but she clung on until the storm passed. As the blood-red sun sank below a sea of cloud, she spied the mystic's hovel, perched like an eagle's eyrie among the crags ...

It was beginning to get dark when Skinner told Vonnie to fetch the bathroom scales and meet him on the patio in the back garden. There was a damp feel and a damp smell to the air. Skinner was standing by the coal bunker near the fence. The lounge-room curtains were still open and she could see Mam sitting on the sofa watching telly.

"Put the scales down there," said Skinner. "Gently. No, not on the sack. Over there a bit. That's it. Now grab the sack and hold it open."

Vonnie saw that all the coal had been removed from the coal bunker and piled against the fence. While she held open the old potato sack, Skinner picked up some of the bigger pieces of coal and lowered them in. She knew better than to question what he was doing.

"Right, I'll have it now," he said.

He hoisted the sack onto the bathroom scales and waited for it to settle.

"Hmm, five stone four pounds," he said.

He took a pencil and notebook from his boiler-suit pocket and jotted down his findings. Then he hauled the sack to waist-height and emptied it into the coal bunker. A cloud of dust billowed out and twinkled a little in the light from the kitchen and lounge windows. Vonnie got a faceful of it before she had a chance to step back.

"Next one," said Skinner.

She held the sack open for him again and considered the big heap of coal against the fence. They could be out here for quite some time, she realised, and she was already starting to feel cold in just a tee-shirt.

"Come on," said Skinner. "Wake up. You're letting it go all floppy. How am I supposed to – ? That's better."

Half an hour and nine sack-loads later, Skinner was sweating and Vonnie's teeth were chattering.

"Er, I might just nip in and get a jumper," she said.

"Nah, don't worry about that. We're nearly finished."

Vonnie said nothing, although she could see that at least half of the coal by the fence still remained. Skinner produced a pen and notebook and did some calculations. His tongue curled out from his mouth as he wrote.

"Work like a Trojan all day, I can," he said. "The rest of 'em at Stannitons don't know what hard work is. That's why the gaffers put me on the Capstan."

Vonnie didn't know what a Capstan looked like, but understood that it was an engineering machine of some kind. She imagined him sweating all day, running up and down catwalks, checking gauges and adjusting levers.

"I just keep going," he said. "Stop for no-one. Most of the blokes there are soft as babies' bums. They don't come nowhere near me. I'm sort of in this special room with the Capstan, see. It's got windows all round it. I can see the rest of the workshop, but I'm divided off from it. I prefer it anyway. They're all scum, that lot. Lazy and sneaky. You never know what they might be saying behind your back. Especially that long-haired git with the 'tache. Can't trust him an inch. You can't trust anybody really. I'm sure that new coalman fiddled us on the last delivery. Well, he's not getting away with it this time! Right. Where were we?"

"Uh ... don't know," said Vonnie.

Skinner studied the figures in the notebook.

"That makes it six-and-a-half hundredweight, near as damn it. Mind you, did I write the last one down?"

"Yes," said Vonnie quickly.

"You sure? What was it then? What was the weight?"

"Er, four stone ... something?"

"Nah, that was the one before the last."

"Oh ... was it?"

Skinner looked at the heap of coal still left against the fence and then peered into the coal bunker; he scratched his head and considered the figures in his notebook again; then he turned on Vonnie.

"That's you, that is."

"What?"

"You. Whining on about wanting to go in the house to get a jumper. You've made me forget where we were."

"Uh ... I didn't mean to."

48

Vonnie stared at her blackened hands. She glanced through the window into the lounge where Mam was laughing at something on telly.

"Come on," said Skinner. "We'll have to start again."

Involuntarily, Vonnie laughed.

"I'm not joking," he said. "Jump in."

"Jump ... ? What?"

"In the coal bunker. Start passing the big bits out to me. I was in there for half an hour before you even came out here. Come on. We'll work faster. Soon have it done."

"Yeah ... I'm so cold," she said.

Skinner took his old jacket down from where it was hanging on a fence post.

"Here. Use this."

Vonnie put the jacket on and swung one leg over the side of the coal-bunker.

Another hour later, she was holding the sack open and Skinner was finally shovelling up the last of the grit and dust from the patio. He aimed the shovelful into the sack and a great filthy plume rose into the air.

While Skinner hauled the sack onto the bathroom scales, Vonnie backed away across the patio towards the kitchen window, coughing and rubbing her eyes.

"I can taste it," she said.

"*Bon appetit*," said Skinner.

He did some calculations in his notebook.

"It's a total of exactly twelve hundredweight," he said.

"Er, how much did you order?" she said.

"Twelve hundredweight."

Vonnie heard a noise behind her and turned to see Mam coming around the corner of the house with a tray of biscuits and cups of tea.

"About time," said Skinner. He snatched a cup from the tray and took a swallow. "Luke warm. And it tastes disgusting. What did you make it with, dishwater?"

Mam made another of her warbling laughs.

49

"Honestly, Bill. How's yours, Vonnie? And look at the state of you. You look like the coalman's son."

"She does," said Skinner, cramming a gingernut into his mouth. "I'll tell you what, though – she'd be halfway pretty if she grew her hair and wore a dress."

Another cream cake with dirt in the middle, thought Vonnie – except that she wasn't going to eat this one.

8

Champagne & Bonfires

... The mystic came out of his hovel in the mountain crags and looked Agata up and down sceptically. He read her KICK ME sign. He nodded slowly. Instead of kicking her, the mystic made some strange herbal tea and invited her to tell her story.

When he'd heard everything, he took a piece of charcoal between his ancient fingers, and with a crafty gleam in his yellow eyes, he added a single word to Agata's sign: DON'T.

Agata was very happy as she trekked back down the mountainside to take her place in the world.

Maybe now, even though she was no longer so youthful, a tradesman might still engage her as an apprentice. It wasn't too late for her. She may yet find the key to her life ...

A few days after the coal-weighing episode, it was Guy Fawkes Night. At home straight after school, Vonnie made herself a quick sandwich and went up to her room to listen to records. Mam was doing a late shift at the hospital and Skinner was giving his beloved Zodiac an oil-change. He'd always hated Bonfire Night; he usually moaned about it a lot and kept the windows shut.

Vonnie had played Simon & Garfunkel's 'Bridge Over Troubled Water' four times before she realised that she was sinking into a gloomy mood.

At the record player, she sorted through her singles and set five more vinyl 45s on the mechanism at the top of the spindle. She operated the play switch. The first disc dropped onto the turntable and the stylus arm traversed into position. 'Lola' by the Kinks helped to cheer her up a bit, and the rest of the cheering up was supplied by Bob and Marcia singing 'Young, Gifted and Black', a cover of an original Nina Simone song. Vonnie didn't stay to hear any more of the records she'd selected because she was suddenly filled with the desire to get out of the house.

She left her bike behind and walked again. It made her feel more connected with the stone-mason's daughter in a way, giving her the sense of travelling the land on foot, always looking for answers.

Dusk was falling as she crossed the Twicken and skirted the edge of the woods. She played 'Lola' over in her head and sang some of the lyrics out loud.

"Well, we drank champagne and danced all night ..."

Vonnie thought it would be really amazing and grown-up and such a groovy thing to do, drinking champagne and dancing all night with a special friend. She pictured herself dancing under colourful strobe-lights with Matt, but it didn't feel quite right. Matt morphed into Dawn, but that didn't feel quite right either.

By the time she reached Horsefair Road, the streetlamps were flickering on and a fog was rolling in from the woods. In the twilight, the odd early rocket fizzled skywards.

Vonnie turned her collar up and pulled her woolly hat down more tightly on her head. When she reached Main Street, many of the shopfronts were still lit, although it was nearly closing-time. A colourful poster in the window of the newsagent was advertising fireworks. She nipped inside and went straight to the sweet counter near the till.

"Are Flying Saucers still ha'pence for two, Mr Thorpe?" she asked, pointing at them beneath the glass.

"Yes, duck," said Bert Thorpe. "How many do you want? Quick, mind. I'm about to close. As they come as well; there's no time to pick colours."

"Six, please."

"Three ha'p'orth," he muttered to himself as he scooped the sweets into a little conical white paper bag.

"There you go. That's three ha'pence."

Vonnie paid and left, then walked along the foggy street smiling to herself. "Three ha'pence" was so old-fashioned. Most people would say "a penny-ha'penny". She wondered how he'd cope with Decimalisation next February when the old coins disappeared. The smallest new coin would be a half-new-pence, which was equivalent to one-and-a-bit old pennies, or exactly 1.2 – they'd worked it out at school.

Like most other children she knew, Vonnie was looking forward to decimal money, but she knew that a lot of older people were worried. The advice being given on telly adverts and information shorts was to "*think* Decimal".

Vonnie popped a Flying Saucer in her mouth, sucked on the rice-paper shape until it went soggy, then bit into it so that the sherbet flooded her mouth.

She almost didn't recognise Rick up ahead. There were two figures in hats, talking in the middle of the pavement, one with a child in a pushchair. A big dog that seemed to be with them lolloped about nearby. It could have been a family. Then Vonnie saw that the dog was Killer.

As she got nearer, one of the figures – a stooped old man in a flat cap – handed something over and turned away. The remaining figure was Rick in a pom-pom hat, and the "child" in the pushchair was a guy. It was a pretty good guy, too, with boots and gloves and bits of straw sticking out from the cuffs, and a creepy green Guy Fawkes mask.

"Hi, Rick," said Vonnie.

Rick looked down for a second, then back up. He was still slightly wary of her since she'd got the better of him in the brief scrap they'd had in the summer.

"Hi, Vonnie. What you up to?"

"Just hanging about."

A woman walked past and Rick shot after her.

"Got a penny for the guy, missus?" he said.

"I've not, love. Sorry."

Suddenly, the guy came to life! It leaped out of the pushchair, groaning hideously, and went straight for Vonnie. She stumbled backwards and nearly choked on a Flying Saucer she was still sucking and chewing. Killer ran in circles about the pavement, howling.

Then Badger took the mask off and laughed.

"Soz if I scared you," he said. "It's what we've been doing if we see anyone we know."

"You loons," said Vonnie. She laughed and said, "How much have you made?"

"It's been a bit rubbish tonight," said Rick.

"Yeah," said Badger. "But we got nearly seven shillings last night. Nidge, Matt and Eddie were here. It was a great laugh. Then we saw my brother, right, and he went in the shop for us and got loads of air-bombs and bangers."

"Yeah!" said Rick. "We took 'em straight over the park and let 'em off. But this bobby on a bicycle turned up and started telling us off, so we had to leg it."

"I heard about that this afto," said Vonnie. "So where's everyone tonight?"

"Dunno," said Rick. "It's Bonny Night anyway. Nidge and Eddie were here earlier. Matt's got to stay in. His sister's boyfriend's going 'round to meet the family."

Vonnie nodded. She offered the Flying Saucers around and Rick and Badger took one each.

A teenaged couple walked past holding hands.

"Penny for the guy?" Rick called out.

"What guy?" the girl said over her shoulder as she and her boyfriend carried on walking.

Rick, Badger and Vonnie looked at one another, looked at the empty pushchair, then laughed.

"What guy?" said Vonnie.

"Yeah, what guy?" said Rick.

"What guy?" said Badger.

And every time they'd started to settle down, one of them would say "What guy?" and they'd stagger about the pavement laughing again.

When they'd finally settled down, Rick and Badger shuffled their feet and made to go – they had sausage cobs and bonfire toffee and fireworks waiting at their houses.

"Er ... just a sec," said Vonnie. "Do either of you know Matt's phone number?"

"Yeah," said Rick. "It's 4722."

"Thanks. See you tomorrow."

"See you," they both said.

The smell of bonfires was starting to drift through the streets. It was getting foggier and darker by the minute, and Vonnie already knew that she'd have to avoid even the edge of the woods and the Twicken and take the long way home. She crossed the road and went into the phone box on the corner of Main Street and Hawker Street.

She picked up the Bakelite receiver, dialled the number and fed her pennies in the slot when the pips sounded.

"Hello?" said a woman with a posh voice. *"Blackthorn 4722. Who's calling?"*

"Er, does Matt Baxter live there?"

"Mathew? Yes, dear. Can I ask who's calling?"

Vonnie thought Matt lived in the terraced houses on Grebble Road, but after hearing his mother's voice, she wondered if maybe they lived in one of the big detached places with the long front gardens on Fairfield Way.

"Er, hello," said Vonnie. "Can I speak to him? Er, if he's there. It's ... a friend from school."

"Oh, yes. Hold on, dear. I'll see if he's in."

She heard a muffled voice followed by a girl and a boy's laughter. Was it a trick? Had she set herself up in some way by asking Matt's friends for his number? Vonnie moved the receiver away from her ear and hesitated, torn between waiting or hanging up.

9

The Best Room

Matt couldn't believe he was missing out on penny-for-the-guy because his soppy sister had brought her soppy boyfriend to the house. Mike lived in London and they'd met at the Isle of Wight festival. Jenny had been singing in the bathroom lately and exuding cheerfulness wherever she went. It was beyond embarrassing.

"Here we go," said Mum, wheeling in a tin trolley that Matt hadn't seen in years. "Coffee made with milk."

"Coffee?" said Dad.

"I thought it'd be nice," said Mum as she began handing the drinks around.

"Cups and saucers?" said Dad. "We expecting royalty?"

"Ignore him, Mike," said Mum.

"Just making extra work for yourself," said Dad.

"Behave, Ron. Nothing wrong with working to make things nice. That reminds me, Mathew. Talking about work. A new woman started as supervisor in packing this week. Seems nice. Jan, her name is. She's got a daughter, Dawn Hagley. Very pretty. Jan showed me a photo. In the same year as you at the Modern School. Jan said they moved to Blackthorn over the summer. Buying a house up on the Willowbank Estate. Wondered if you know her?"

"Willowbank Estate?" said Matt. "What road do they live on? What number?"

"Oh, I don't know ... Do you know her then?"

"What? Er, no. No."

In the big armchair by the front window, Dad made slurping sounds as he drank coffee from the saucer. Mum watched in horror as he tipped more into the saucer from the willow-pattern cup, blew on it, swilled it around and then slurped again.

"Ron!"

"What?"

"Manners."

"Eh, what do you mean? It's too hot straight from the cup. What do you expect me to do?"

Jenny sniggered and shuffled closer to Mike on the sofa. Matt poured coffee into his saucer and slurped at it.

"Mathew!"

"Dad's doing it."

"Stop, both of you. Please. I'm sure Mike doesn't want to see this sort of behaviour. It's like having the chimpanzees here from that PG Tips advert."

Matt thought back to when he'd seen Mike on the park with Jenny. They'd all been sitting on the grass, smoking and passing wine around, drinking it from the bottle. Mike was being very polite today. His long hair and beard looked freshly washed and his jeans and psychedelic shirt looked new. Disappointingly, he didn't have his guitar.

It was loony-tunes that Mum had insisted on being in the front room, or Best Room as it was known. Nobody ever usually used it, except to leave the house by the street door, or to make or answer phone calls. There was no telly, and every wall was lined with dark edifices of furniture that had belonged to Dad's dead parents.

There was nothing to do in the Best Room but stare into the tiled hearth and the empty fire-grate.

"Can we put some music on?" he said.

Mum looked uncertainly towards the huge gramophone that sat under the front window like a sarcophagus.

"Well," she said. "It depends what music."

"My new single, 'Paranoid' by Black Sabbath," said Matt. "I'll go upstairs and get it."

"Ooh no," said Mum.

"Why not?"

"They sound like devil-worshippers. Horrible!"

"Or some Led Zeppelin."

"I'm sure Mike wants to listen to something nice," said Mum. "Don't you, Mike?"

"I'm fine with anything, Mrs Baxter."

Mum went to the gramophone and lifted the lid.

"Stick some Elvis on," said Dad.

"Maybe later," said Mum. "Oh, here we go."

Matt couldn't see what she was putting on but he was already feeling embarrassed. Why couldn't Mike have voted for Sabbath? But he knew that Mike probably didn't like Sabbath much. Matt had heard the records Jenny had been borrowing from Mike – The Doors, Jimi Hendrix, Family, Joni Mitchell – and, yeah, they were all really groovy sounds, but Matt and Nidge preferred heavy rock.

A few seconds later, Sacha Distel was singing 'Raindrops Keep Fallin' On My Head'.

Matt covered his ears.

"I don't care what you think, Mathew," said Mum. "I like it. It's catchy. And it's decent. Do you like it, Mike?"

"Mum ..." said Jenny.

"Oh, yes, Mrs Baxter," said Mike. "It's quite different from what I usually listen to and .... What I mean is ... But I have to say that, *in its own way*, it has a kind of – "

"See," said Mum, looking around smugly at Dad, Matt and Jenny. "Even Mike likes it."

Mike frowned and took a delicate sip from his cup.

"Your job sounds interesting, Mrs Baxter," he said. "The packing department, did you say?"

"Oh, it's just the local biscuit factory," she said. "I probably won't be there much longer. It's temporary until I find something better."

"Temporary?" said Dad. "You've been there nigh on twenty years. What else are you going to do? Like they say, the only way out of Wedderburn's is the golden handshake or in a pine box. Same as my job on the railway."

"Jack left the biscuit factory years ago," said Mum.

"Granted," said Dad. "And he's been on and off the dole ever since." He turned to Mike. "Jack's Dot's brother. Nice enough bloke, but he's a bit *dainty*."

"He just hasn't found a job that suits him," said Mum.

"Is that why Aunt Mavis left him?" said Matt.

"Well ... they were never very well suited."

"He didn't know what hit him," said Dad. "Nobody saw him for months. Then he got that motorbike and started dressing like a teenager. All them bell-bottomed trousers and women's shirts. He looks as if he's raided Jenny's wardrobe half the time ..."

He stopped because Jenny was glaring at him, and Mike was looking uncomfortable.

"Good worker, mind you, Jack is," said Dad. "He came to work on the railway once. Anyway, people can wear whatever clothes they like. No skin off my nose."

"Yeah," said Jenny. "None of us ever laughed at you when you used to put your Teddy boy clobber on."

"Still do, now and then, when there's a good rock 'n' roll band on at the club. Like I say, people can wear what they like. Look at that Danny La Rue. Blokes in women's clothes all over the place in London, are there, Mike?"

"Soho's pretty good that way," said Mike. "Relaxed. I'm the same as you, Mr Baxter; I think everybody should be allowed to do their own thing."

"Ron. Call me Ron. What do you do for a job, Mike?"

Matt knew from Jenny that Mike was on the dole. And apart from a couple of short spells in local factories, Jenny had hardly worked during her two years since school.

"He's a song-writer," said Jenny.

"Right," said Dad. "Does it pay the bills? See, if Jenny's moving down to London next year, like she wants – "

"Ron," said Mum.

59

"They need to be able to feed themselves," said Dad.

Mike cleared his throat and leaned forward.

"You don't need to worry," he said. "I do write songs. I don't get paid anything for that. Not yet. We're in the early stage of forming a band. But the house where I live is a commune. Six other couples are there, some with children. There's a large garden and we grow most of our own food. Some have jobs, some are artists, but everybody pays their way or does work to the property or the land."

Dad appeared not to know what to make of this.

On the sofa, Jenny smiled up at Mike and nestled closer to him. He put his arm around her shoulders. Next thing, they were engaged in a really long snog. Matt kept having quick looks because he was curious to see how it was done. Mum and Dad tried to pretend that it wasn't happening, or that it was perfectly normal.

"Look at that fog coming down," said Mum. She went to the window and gazed up and down the street.

As well as taking notes on how to snog, Matt was getting impatient about going out to the yard for the fireworks. Jenny hated fireworks, so he knew that he'd have to wait until Mike had taken her to the pub.

"Right," said Dad, when the snog had ended. "What are your politics, Mike? Don't tell me you voted for Ted Heath back in the summer?"

"Er ... I didn't vote at all, Ron."

"What? We could have done with all the non-voters voting for Wilson. The Tories are a rich man's party. We had a day of Go Slow at the railway depot the day after Heath got in. Just for good measure."

Dad grinned around the room at everybody.

"Up the workers," he said.

Mike smiled politely and started snogging Jenny again.

The telephone rang. Mum went over to where it sat on the dark varnished sideboard.

"Hello?" she said in a posh voice.

"Here we go," said Dad. "Telephone voice."

"Blackthorn 4722," said Mum. "Who's calling?" After a pause, she said, "Mathew? Yes, dear. Can I ask who's calling?" Following a longer pause, she said, "Oh, yes. Hold on, dear. I'll see if he's in."

Mum placed the receiver gently down on the sideboard, looked over at Matt and signalled to him.

"*See if he's in?*" said Dad. "He's sitting right bloody there in front of you."

Jenny and Mike burst into laughter.

"It's for you, Mathew," Mum said quietly. "A girl."

Matt jumped up and went to the sideboard.

Was it Dawn? Had she asked about him and got his number from a friend?

Dad poured the rest of his coffee into the saucer, slurped it up, then said to Mike and Jenny, "I told you we were expecting royalty. Here we are sitting in the Best Room for the first time in about six years, cups and saucers, Dot putting on her posh voice for the telephone ..."

Matt cupped his hand over the ear-piece.

"Er, hi," he said. "It's Matt."

"*Hi, Matt. Vonnie.*"

"Vonnie? Oh."

"*I got your number from Rick.*"

"Yeah, okay. You having a good Bonny Night?"

"*Er, no. We don't do it. My stepdad ...*"

She went quiet then. Matt didn't know what to say. He heard the crumps and bangs of fireworks from a nearby yard and was desperate to set off his own with Dad.

"*I wanted to ask you ...*" said Vonnie.

"Yeah?"

"*About the shack. Is it nearly finished?*"

"Shack?" he said. "Oh ... yeah. It's ... it needs a bit more work. I've got all the posts in and one – no, two of the sides done. It's gonna be magic."

"*Great. I could help you with it, if you want?*"

61

"No! I mean, what it is ... I prefer to work on my own."
"Okay. Groovy. Let me know when it's ready."
"Yeah, will do."

Matt put the receiver down and felt ashamed. He'd lied to Vonnie and he wasn't even sure why.

"What's her name?" said Mum. "Is she in your class at the Modern School?"

"Uh ... it was a wrong number," said Matt.

10

Shady Lane

The next day was Friday, and as Matt dawdled home after school he marvelled at the fallen, burn-out husks of some of the more expensive-looking rockets. He collected the best ones and took them home with him.

Bonfire Night had been what Dad termed "a wash-out". No sooner had Jenny and Mike gone off to the pub than the sky had opened and the rain had bucketed down. Dad had persevered, lighting the fireworks and sheltering in the outside toilet to watch them with Matt.

The outside toilet was where Matt now stowed the spent rockets. He had a pee while he was in there. It was as he was pulling the chain to flush it that he cast his eyes over the shelf on the wall near the rusty cistern. Some old tools were stored up there. He found a claw-hammer and a bag of six-inch nails. Encouraged, he had a poke around outside in the yard and found two old fence posts being digested beneath a bed of stinging nettles.

Further back in the narrow yard – half buried under more weeds and some rubble from the broken-down garden wall – Matt could see a handlebar of his bike sticking up. The bike had no chain, no tyres or inner-tubes, no brakes to speak of, and buckled wheels.

He went to the back door, opened it and called out. Dad was home already because he'd been on an early shift.

"Dad? Dad?"

The bedroom window opened.

"What?" Dad called down. "I was about to have a kip."

"Uh, soz."

"What is it?"

"Can I borrow this hammer and nails? And there's some old bits of wood in the yard. Can I have them?"

"What for?"

"I'm making a ... tree house. In the woods."

"Too dangerous. I've told you about climbing trees."

"I know. It's not really a tree house ... It's more like a shack built *under* a tree."

"Where in the woods?" said Dad.

"Probably near Shady Lane somewhere."

"Go on then. It'll be dark in about an hour. Don't be in the woods when it's getting dark."

Matt filled his pockets with nails, tucked the hammer under his arm and lugged the old fence posts along the foot-passage – or "entry" as it was called – which ran like an arched tunnel from the back yards of the terraced houses and out to the pavement. Next door had got some washing hanging on a line on their side of the entry, and the end of Matt's wood got tangled in a bed-sheet. He stopped and tried to wipe the mud off the wet sheet, but his efforts just made it look worse.

Matt hurried on his way.

On Shady Lane, the dominant colours were the greys of the road and sky and the autumn reds and golds of the leaves. It was a late season. Not a single leaf had fallen. The canopy of Blackthorn Woods, stretching out to the south, looked like a blanket of fire.

He spotted the abandoned Austin Cambridge that had been there for at least five years. It sat at an angle across the ditch. Blackberry bushes and young ash-trees already hid the faded grey of its bodywork partially from view. The front passenger seat had been liberated by Matt and Nidge two summers ago. They would have had the driver's seat, too, but the bolts had seized up.

The ditch, which divided the roadside verge from the woods, was thick with stinging nettles, and the easiest crossing-point was through the car. It had started raining now though, so rather than walk any further, Matt threw the posts and tools over the ditch, then took a running jump himself, making it over without getting stung.

The cover of the woods offered immediate shelter, but he knew from experience that once the treetops had soaked up so much, the rain would leak through.

Not far from the road, he came upon an egg-shaped hollow. An ivied elm stood in the centre and there were fallen trunks sprouting leathery toadstools and lime-green mosses and lichens. The earth was soft and springy and it was very cool in the hollow, like an air-conditioned chamber. Matt remembered being there with Nidge once before. Nidge had called the place the Egg Room, saying it would be their secret. And Matt had wondered why anybody would care, since they already had much better dens, but he'd humoured Nidge at the time.

Now, Matt stood in the Egg Room and considered whether it would be a good place for the shack. It seemed doubtful. A flat floor would be needed, not a bowl shape that might become a mud bath in wet weather.

The rain had eased, so he wouldn't be able to see the mud-bath theory put to the test anyway.

Further on, he found a flat, raised area of ground. It had three trees at the perimeter, so positioned that they made the three corners of a rough rectangle.

Perfect!

It was more exposed here, the thinner trees offering less cover, and the rain was picking up again. And, okay, he didn't have all the materials he needed to finish the shack today, but once it was built, it would be in a really good spot and completely weather-proof.

Matt struggled for twenty minutes trying to make a post-hole with the claw-end of the hammer. His efforts were hampered by roots and stones. Another ten minutes, and he'd got the end of a post into a hole that was barely six inches deep. He scraped the loose soil and stones back in and packed it down.

The post stayed there when he let go.

He felt very happy.

Next, he offered up the other post as a cross-member to go at head-height to the nearest tree along the shortest side of the rectangle. It didn't reach. Nowhere near. And now the rain was pouring down again. And the first post had begun to lean over. Matt straightened it and wedged his boot against its base. He rammed an end of the second post against the ground a few feet away and angled it up against the upright post.

Keeping everything in place with his feet, his body and one hand – in what felt like an improvised game of Twister – he fished the bag of nails from his pocket and the hammer from under his arm.

Now he was getting somewhere! After all, you couldn't build a shack in one go. He'd get this corner post secured, using the second post as a strut or something. Then he could bring more wood for the cross-members and sides, and eventually the roof.

Another worry had surfaced though. Here he was preparing a shack in the woods for himself and Vonnie to run away together. So what about Dawn? Did this mean that he was a two-timing git?

The rain got suddenly much heavier and the ground underfoot was already muddy and awash.

It was getting dark.

Balancing and holding everything as well as he could with his legs, feet, body and neck, Matt set a nail against the angled post with one hand and swung the hammer with the other. The hammer missed the nail and skinned his knuckles. He shouted out, but managed to hold on to his lengths of timber and keep them roughly in place. He set another nail against the post, took a swing and ...

Matt and the posts went sideways.

He slid partly down the muddy bank that sloped away from the raised area. For a full minute, he lay there on his back, gazing up at the darkening grey sky through the thin leaf cover, the rain falling steadily into his face and soaking into his clothes. Then he got up and searched for the hammer. It was nowhere to be seen, and the nails were scattered everywhere in the mud.

Matt made his way out of the woods to Shady Lane and walked home in the rain.

"There's just too many prats hanging around with us," said Nidge as an opener to the gang meeting.

It was Saturday, the morning after Matt's attempt to build a shack. A few meetings in HQ had been missed lately, partly because of heavy rain and partly because it was getting dark earlier in the evenings.

The other boys, including Matt, looked around at one another wondering who the "prats" were. Matt knew that it couldn't be him or Rick or Winston or Eddie. They were the core members. Badger was a *bit* of a prat, but he had his uses. So, by Matt's reckoning, the prats had to be Sammy, Boggo, Daz, and Monkey-Breath Mosley. They were all pretty boring, never had much to say for themselves, and were always last to pay their subs.

"We need the numbers though," said Nidge. "Greenie's gang are getting massive. There's about twenty of them now. Right ... so ... Subs are going up to thruppence a week, and we'll start having some kind of fight training. Winston can teach us some of his judo moves."

"I ain't paying thruppence a week," said Daz.

"Get lost then," said Nidge.

Daz and Nidge locked gazes. Matt and the rest sat still and silent for the staring-out match. After about three minutes, Daz got up, straddled his bike and rode off.

Nidge tilted his chin and glanced around the gathering; he seemed slightly awed by his own power.

"Any other gang business?" he said.

"Yeah," said Badger. "I had to do gym in my pants again yesterday."

"So what?" said Eddie. "Don't keep losing your kit."

"I know. I'm just saying. Thommo's a git."

"Did everyone see *UFO* the other night?" said Rick.

"I missed it," said Sammy. "What happened?"

"I saw it," said Matt.

"Yeah," said Badger. "It was a dead good 'un. Called 'Kill Straker!' And it was amazing because Foster and this other bloke, right, they're making a re-entry to Earth and they're being chased by this UFO and then something dead weird happens ... I missed a bit myself then coz that's when when my big brother staggered in, canned-up, and the old man gave him a bollocking – "

"Straker and everybody at SHADO lost contact with the ship," said Matt. "Then the screen was flicking between Foster and his mate and the UFO, and there was an alien voice doing mind control – "

"Yeah," said Badger, "and after they've landed, Foster goes doo-lally and starts trying to kill Straker."

"But he don't get killed," said Winston. "And all the SHADO women on Moonbase Alpha with their silver outfits and purple hair – they were really sexy again. It'd be good if that was the school uniform for girls."

It had started raining again and Nidge was shifting about in the car-seat. He threw a stone into the trees.

"Any more gang business?" he said.

"I saw a UFO once," said Badger.

"No you didn't," said Eddie.

"I did! It was this summer just gone when we were on holiday in a caravan in Skeggy."

"You've not told us about it before," said Eddie.

"No, well, I've only known you lot and only been in the gang since the end of the summer holidays, so I didn't know if you'd even believe me – "

"We don't."

"Eddie, I saw one! I'm telling you. Cub's honour."

"*Cub's honour!* I thought you didn't go no more?"

"I don't. Anyway, I saw one. It was the middle of the night. I woke up in the caravan and everyone else was asleep, right, and I heard this whirring noise and saw these blue lights at the window – "

"A cop car or an ambulance," said Winston.

"No. I thought that myself, but when I got to the window I saw the lights skimming over the sea, and they weren't even blue; they were more like a purple colour. The sun was just coming up as well. Then this UFO just shot up into the sky – *zip!* In about a millionth of a second. It was dead fast, right. I woke my dad up, but it was gone."

"What did it look like?" said Matt.

"Sort of silver, and with purple lights underneath – "

"Silver and purple?" said Eddie. "The same colours as the Moonbase Alpha women's costumes, then?"

"Everyone shut up about UFOs," said Nidge. "We've got to do something about Greenie's gang. They took half a packet of Toffos off Winston yesterday, a Sherbet Fountain off me the day before."

"Did Greenie kiss you?" said Eddie with a snigger.

Nidge glared at Eddie.

"He always kisses you," said Winston. "When they've took your rocks, Greenie kisses you. It's weird."

"What are we going to do?" said Matt.

"I'll think of something," said Nidge.

11

Falling

It rained solid for the rest of the weekend, and carried on raining every day until Thursday. That evening, Vonnie had been watching the chart run-down on *Top of the Pops* when Skinner came in drunk. Melanie was still at No. 9 with her cover of 'Ruby Tuesday', which was okay, but Vonnie thought the Stones original was much better.

Then Skinner fell in a heap near the gas fire.

"Who legged me over?" he grunted.

Mam rushed in from the kitchen.

"Ooh, Bill!" she said, kneeling beside him.

"Where's my dinner?" he slurred.

"It's been in the oven. Shall I heat it up?"

Skinner said something unintelligible.

"Billy?" said Mam.

He began snoring gently into the carpet.

Vonnie got up from the armchair and left the room. She'd missed the rest of the run-down, but she knew from the radio last Sunday that No. 1 was still 'Woodstock' by Mathews' Southern Comfort.

In her bedroom, she stood by the window in darkness. Blackthorn Woods was eerie under the moonlight. Over the last few days, the leaves had finally started falling in the woods and in the streets. It was Vonnie's favourite season. Beautiful, sad, exciting, and a bit frightening – it always felt to her like a time of uncertain departure.

... After thanking the mystic and saying goodbye to him, Agata travelled happily onward with her DON'T

KICK ME sign. At the first town she entered, she was kicked by almost everybody in sight. Beggars and matchstick-sellers kicked her. Women with babes-in-arms kicked her. Children kicked her. People saw her from their windows and came hurrying into the street to kick her. A frail old man – who was blind and had only one leg – managed, somehow, to kick her.

Agata tried another town, and the same thing happened. She couldn't understand why this should be. Her sign now clearly said, DON'T KICK ME.

She went back to the mystic but found him dead.

Out of gratitude – because he had tried to help – she worked hard to gather enough wood for a pyre, and repeated as many words as she could remember from the time, so long ago, of her father's funeral. She threw her sign into the flames. As she watched it burning, she fell into a deep swoon. When she awoke, the sign was back around her neck, as new, and the mystic's funeral pyre had been reduced to ashes ...

"Are you all right, Vonnie?" said Mam, sticking her head around the door. "Oh, you're reading. That's nice."

Vonnie had been lying on the bed. Now she sat up.

"Can't we just leave home, Mam?" she said.

Mam came and sat on the edge of the bed. She smiled sadly and took Vonnie's hand.

"We can't just leave home. It doesn't work like that."

"How *does* it work?" said Vonnie.

"I ... don't know."

"Is he still dossed out on the floor?"

"Still asleep on the floor," said Mam. She sighed. "I was going to ask you ... We should try to get him upstairs to bed between us. He won't be very happy if he wakes up downstairs on the floor."

"Whose fault's that?"

"I know, love. Still, we have to do the right thing."

"Why can't we just leave him there, eating carpet, like he deserves? And pack our bags and go?"

Mam laughed softly.

"Go where? We've got no money of our own. No other family. And anyway ... I know Bill has his ups and downs, and his little ways, but honestly, Vonnie, he's nowhere near as bad as your real dad was. You've no idea what I had to put up with when we were with your real dad. And you don't need to know about it either."

"Why not?"

"Oh, you're too young to understand."

"I'm twelve in January. Did he used to hit you?"

"He did, love. Yes."

"Has Skinner ever hit you?"

Mam looked down.

"Listen, Vonnie. When we left your real dad, we had somewhere to go. Bill was really kind to us. I knew him from when he was a patient ... he was brought in by ambulance after a car accident – "

"What? Drunk?"

"Oh, I don't know about that. He was lucky to be alive though. He was on my ward for three weeks, and we got talking ... Anyway, about six months afterwards, I bumped into him while I was shopping at the market. We had a drink together, then met a few times again after that, and he was really sympathetic. I'd told him about your dad, and he said I should leave and that you'd be welcome as well. You were only two at the time."

"Then we came here."

"Yes. So he was really good to us."

"What time of year was it?"

"Autumn. Similar time to now."

"Thought so," said Vonnie. "I remember the leaves."

"You were only two."

"I do. I remember the falling leaves everywhere."

"Bill was really good to us."

"He's not good to us now."

"Well … he doesn't drink as much as your dad did."

"Dad died from booze, didn't he? Drank even more after we left him. Then one night, he puked his guts up in his sleep and couldn't wake up because he was so drunk and he choked to death on the puke."

"How did you – ?"

"Heard you telling some woman in town years ago."

"Hmm. Well, thankfully Bill doesn't drink that much."

"He still drinks a lot. And treats you like a doormat. He makes me weed the garden when it's raining – always when it's raining. And wash his car with that sponge that's falling to bits. And he never lets me have any friends here, and I haven't got any friends because he hates everyone. We can't even answer the door like normal people. He's a selfish pig and a bully. Horrible to us, and never even calls us by our names! Mam, please let's go away."

"Vonnie, I – "

"What if there was a place? A place that was a bit rough and not very comfortable? But it was somewhere we could stay until we worked out what to do? I don't know, some shack in the woods or something?"

Mam laughed.

"A shack in the woods? Listen, love. One day, all right? One day, we'll go away properly. You and me."

"Really? When? Soon?"

"Maybe in a few years. When I can save some money."

"*A few years?*"

"In a few years, we'll see what … Oh, look at the time! I'm late. Quick, love. Please … we'll get him upstairs to bed and then I'll have to run for the bus on the corner."

Mam was already on her feet, looking back from the bedroom doorway. Vonnie stood.

"You've got to go in?" she said, following Mam out to the landing and the stairs.

"Sorry, love."

"I thought you'd finished with late shifts for a while?"

"This is an extra shift. They needed me."

In the lounge, Skinner had rolled onto his back and was snoring loudly.

"Just leave him there," said Vonnie. "I don't care. I'll just go back up to my room."

"I'd feel better if we got him upstairs and on the bed. If he wakes up on the floor in the middle of the night ... It'll put him in a bad mood tomorrow."

Between them, they lifted him into a sitting position; then, as he roused a little and became semi-conscious, Mam talked him into helping them.

"I told him ..." he said, as they guided him out to the hall, "... long-haired git with the 'tache ... told him ... keep your filthy maulers off my micra ... mico ... micrometers, and my depth-gauges. Must have sneaked in again ..."

Halfway up the stairs, he slumped heavily against the wall. From behind, Mam managed to stop both him and herself falling backwards.

Vonnie got a faceful of beer breath as he spoke to her.

"What d'you think you're doing?" he slurred, eyes out of focus. "Where's your mother? I know your little games ... think you can get the better of me ... No! You won't!"

"We're just trying to help you," said Vonnie.

"What's that? The only help I want from you ... yeah, yeah ... no idea what it's like for me ... nobody does. See, your mother ... only ever cares about what *she* wants. And you! No respect. Don't know the meaning of it."

He leaned closer to her. A vein was pulsing at his temple and his lips were curled over his teeth.

"Teach *you* some respect. One night when your mother's on a late. Little talk about respect. My old man ... he'd take his belt off to me. Do you the world of good, that would."

Vonnie's breath caught in her throat. She shuddered and sat back heavily on the stair behind her. She felt as if her mind was being consumed by darkness. Why couldn't Mam see how dangerous things were getting?

"Don't you ever hit me," she said quietly.

"What's that? Get out the way. Can get up the stairs by myself. Where's the ... where's your mother? Never around when she's wanted. Probably at work ... flirting with all the patients on the men's ward. Is that what the two of you talk about behind my back? Does she think I'm an idiot? I ever catch you ... bash your brains in. The pair of you. Acting all suspicious ... You think I don't know what's going on ... Semolina pudding? More like gammon and sprouts. I'm not an idiot. Where's your mother?"

"Right behind you, Bill," said Mam. "Holding you up."

"I know that!" he said. "I'm not stupid!"

"No. You're not stupid."

Skinner flailed his arms. Vonnie and Mam dodged out of the way, and Skinner saved himself from falling backwards by grabbing the bannister.

"Parasites, the pair of you," he said.

As he stood swaying on the stairs, a wet patch spread slowly over the front of his trousers and a smile crept slowly over his face. He looked up at Vonnie.

"Think I need the toilet," he said.

Fifteen minutes later, Skinner was lying on top of the bed asleep, fully clothed, and Mam had gone for the bus. Vonnie got her bike out of the garage and cycled half a mile to the nearest phone box. Skinner could easily have afforded to have one in the house, but he flatly refused.

Inside the damp phone-box that smelled of fag-smoke and stale urine, Vonnie picked up the handset and dialled. She fed her pennies in when the pips sounded.

"*Hello?*" came a familiar, fake-posh voice from the other end of the line. "*Blackthorn 4722. Who's calling?*"

When Matt came to the phone, Vonnie immediately said, "Hi, Matt. The shack? Is it nearly ready?"

"Er ... hi, Vonnie. Yeah ... yeah. Just needs a roof on."

"Is it big enough to have two rooms?"

"Er, yeah. We could divide it off."

"Groovy."

"Yeah."

"Mam's got some old curtains we don't use. They're really big and heavy. They'd make a really good partition. If you can fix up a rod or something across the middle?"

"Yeah, I can do that."

"Matt ... how long before it's ready?"

"Er, say, another week? No, say two weeks."

As Vonnie cycled home, she felt much better. Mam would take a bit more convincing, she knew. But the way Vonnie saw it – if she moved into the shack first and got their room organised, she could go and see Mam at the hospital one school lunchtime and tell her the good news.

12

The Wonder Of Him

At four o'clock on a Tuesday afternoon nearly three weeks later – the beginning of December – Matt and Nidge sat at a favourite spot on the railway embankment.

They were gorging themselves on pop and sweets bought with the sub-money extorted from the others. A quarter of a mile away, shimmering in the exhaust haze, they could see the cars and lorries and buses passing over the bridge like beads running along a wire.

Later, at home, Matt slouched on the settee reading an American comic-book, *Strange Tales*. Dad was watching an old film on telly called *G. I. Blues* and Mum was clattering crockery in the kitchen.

"Thought *you* were supposed to be doing the washing-up tonight?" said Dad.

"Mum likes doing it," said Matt. "Why have we got this crappy old film on anyway?"

Dad gave him a warning glare.

"Bloody class, Elvis is," said Dad.

"Yeah, but rock 'n' roll's dead and buried. Teddy boys and everything all went out yonks ago. Me and Nidge and everyone, we're into bands like Deep Purple and Jethro Tull, Zeppelin, Sabbath ..."

He stopped talking as the phone rang in the front room.

Dad grunted and shifted in his armchair protractedly, as if in preparation to stand up. Then Mum came through from the kitchen and continued to the front room.

"I was about to get that," said Dad.

"If it's for me, I'm not here," said Matt.

He'd been avoiding Vonnie at school recently in case she asked about the shack again.

A few minutes later, Mum came back in.

"It was Jack," she said. "Just to say he's dropping in tomorrow." She knelt by the hearth to put some coal on the dwindling red glow in the grate; then she stood in the middle of the room with her hands on her hips.

"Any cuppas wanted before I sit down?"

Matt and Dad both grunted their affirmations and she headed back to the kitchen. Dad's film had finished and the credits were rolling up.

"That's got me in the mood now, that has," he said.

He crossed to the telly and turned it off.

"*Monty Python*'s starting soon," said Matt.

Dad went into the front room and Matt heard him lifting the creaky lid of the gramophone. A minute later, Elvis was singing 'The Wonder Of You', which had been at number one in the charts for ages in the summer. Dad left the door to the front room open when he came back in.

"Oh, this is nice," said Mum, appearing with the cuppas. "Can we have Sacha Distel next or some Andy Williams?"

"Yeah," said Dad. "Been meaning to tell you, Dot – do you remember that rock 'n' roll group you liked last year? Rock-It, they were called. They're back on again at the club on Saturday. Sid and his missus are going, and Archie. Few drinks, few jives. Fancy it?"

"I don't know, Ron," she said, setting the cups down on the mantelpiece over the fire.

Dad became animated, his face lit with a boyish grin.

"We'll get all the old gear out!"

Matt remembered how Dad used to have his hair done in a D.A., and how Mum had once been equally excited about going to see rock 'n' roll groups.

"You must be joking," she said, clasping her hands over her apron. "The skirt hasn't fit for about five years. And I can't imagine ever jiving again."

"What? Why not? What about Sid's missus? She's on the club dance-floor every chance she gets. In stockings and suspenders, showing everything she's got. You look a sight better than her."

Mum's face had a caved-in appearance.

"I should hope so too," she said.

"Well, that's what I said, ain't it?"

"It's that place," said Mum. "There's always a fight."

Matt had found an old pencil down the side of the sofa cushion. He put the end of it in his mouth and made it spin by rolling it in his fingers; he could taste the cold tang of lead on the tip of his tongue.

"Not that time we saw Rock-It. There's never any fights when rock 'n' roll groups are playing. We sat with Sid and Barbara and Archie. Few drinks, few dances. You enjoyed yourself. You *said* you did. Chatting away with Barbara like you was best mates, far as I remember."

"I was being polite. I don't even like Barbara. And there *was* a fight the night we saw Rock-It. That loud-mouthed bloke from the flats was scrapping with somebody and they fell right across a table of drinks."

"Okay," said Dad, scratching his stubbly chin, "but that was right at the back. It was nowhere near us."

"It's the money, too," said Mum. "I was hoping we might do something about this room soon."

Dad swivelled his head, surveying the smoke-yellowed ceiling and the floral wallpaper peeling at the edges.

"Well, we've not won Where's The Ball *yet*, in case you hadn't noticed."

Matt sometimes helped with the weekly competition that appeared in the *Blackthorn Herald*. There was an action photograph taken from a football match – the ball magicked out of the picture somehow – and you looked at the players' feet and the directions of their gazes and marked crosses where you thought the ball was.

"It wouldn't cost much," said Mum.

"Pull the other one."

"Probably about the same as a night at the club, if the truth's known."

"What? A couple of Barley Wines for you and a couple of pints of bitter for me?"

"A couple?"

"You show me decorating materials for that price and I'll do the room up for you."

"Well, there's a new place in town. I'll have a look."

"What? Oh ... So what about the club on Saturday?"

"I don't know, Ron. I don't really fancy it."

"I'll go by myself then."

"You do that."

"Bloody will do, don't worry."

Matt watched as Mum went back to the kitchen and closed the door. His parents rarely argued, and it didn't seem very serious because Dad gave him a wink.

"Women!" he said. "You'll find out one day."

Matt laughed and swung his feet onto the settee.

He tried to read his comic book again, but had lost interest. His eyes wandered over the floral wallpaper and he found himself playing the old game of picking out imaginary faces – sad and happy, beautiful and ugly, some occupying the same area of wall but transforming themselves at his whim, depending on what perspective or focus he chose, so that in an instant the smiling cherubic mouth of one face could shift shape to become the sickle eye of a demonic other.

The next day, everything seemed to be going Matt's way. He came top in a maths test in the morning, then he met Nidge and everyone at the chip shop at lunchtime, after they'd paid Debbie Moyes to palm all their dinner cards into the collection box on her way in.

The afternoon started with a Games period, which Matt had been dreading. It was a new idea that once a month, the boys' and girls' groups would be mixed up for joint lessons in trampoline, dance or field events.

Matt's group was with Mrs Orton for trampoline in the main gym. The boys were in their usual kit; the girls were in shorts or tracksuit bottoms rather than P.E. skirts. Matt was just considering faking a stomach ache to get out of it when he noticed that Dawn was among the girls.

She had her dark hair tied back in a long pony-tail that swished about when she walked. Although she never looked directly at him, every time *he* looked at *her*, she cast her eyes down and had a little smile on her face.

While each pupil took a turn, everybody else had to stand around the edge of the trampoline.

"All right, Brown," said Mrs Orton. "Just remember what I said: it's not playtime; you have to learn things. I want you to bounce in a controlled way, work up a good height, and then try to do a somersault."

"Yes, Mrs Orton," said the boy on the trampoline.

When it was Dawn's turn, Matt watched her so closely that he barely blinked. He wondered if she'd fancy him if he told her he was going to join the army when he was older? The uniform had seemed to do the trick for Elvis in Dad's film. Matt didn't really like the idea of joining the army, though, so he pictured himself playing the guitar and singing to her.

When it was his turn on the trampoline, he focussed on his feet and tried to do everything perfectly, but his eyes kept seeking out Dawn. His somersault attempt ended in an awkward landing, and in getting bounced face-first against the springs at the edge.

Dawn and her friend jumped back.

"Is he the one?" said the friend.

"Yeah," said Dawn, her face expressionless.

The one? thought Matt excitedly. *The one.*

"The weirdo with the chin," added Dawn.

Her friend giggled.

"Baxter," said Mrs Orton. "You're not concentrating. That could have been really dangerous. Imagine if you'd landed on top of somebody. Try again."

During the last period of the day, Matt was still feeling stung by Dawn's words. It must be true. His chin stuck out just like he'd always known it did, and everybody was laughing at him. Dawn was laughing at him.

The weirdo with the chin.

He tried to convince himself that he'd misheard; he played around with the words and sounds until he came up with *The wonder of him.*

Unusually, Mr Warrilow was running late for history and they had a student teacher, Miss Bloor, who'd been helping out in the class since the beginning of term.

"We're going to start by recapping," she said, "on the differences between London buildings before and after the Great Fire of 1666. As we know, it was all timber frames and wattle-and-daub, buildings of six or seven storeys, and jettied gables overhanging narrow streets ..."

Matt tried to focus. He knew that as soon as Warrilow arrived there would be a test.

"... the legislation for rebuilding London had all sorts of restrictions. Streets had to be wide enough to act as a fire-break. All buildings had to be brick or stone ..."

As part of the long study, Warrilow had overseen the construction of a model – a typical London street in the days before the Great Fire. It had two rows of multi-storeyed houses with black-and-white facades, and was made entirely from matchsticks that had been collected at Warrilow's church, where he was the Sunday school teacher. All the pupils in Blackthorn Modern's history groups had sat for lesson after lesson, with piles of dead matches and tubes of Bostik. The model was mounted on a sheet of plywood, which occupied a low table in the centre of the room. Except for painting the last of the

Tudor facades, the model was complete. Warrilow had even got the metalwork teacher to make an engraved brass plaque that said: BUILT BY FIRST-FORM PUPILS OF BLACKTHORN SECONDARY MODERN, AUTUMN TERM, 1970.

"And the new legislation decreed that there were to be limits to the number of storeys ..."

Matt hoped that Warrilow wouldn't come in at all. He was in the middle of a delicious fantasy about a real fire consuming the model when something small and hard stung him across the cheek. He looked around in time to see Kev Glover lowering a pea-shooter. Kev Glover was one of Greenie's gang, who – although mostly second-formers – had now recruited a few first-formers, like Kev, and even a third-former.

A game of Hangman was being played by the pair of girls at the desk in front of Matt, and at other desks conversations were growing louder and louder.

"There's far too much talking going on," said Miss Bloor. "Can you all please – "

"*I'm* not talking, Miss Bloor," said one boy.

"*I'm* not talking," said another.

"*I'm* not talking either," said a girl.

Then almost everybody repeated the words over and over, like a mantra, until Miss Bloor was sitting at the front desk with her hands covering her ears.

Kev Glover took the opportunity to fire more peas at Matt. One zinged into his neck. It really hurt. Matt leaped to his feet and crossed to Kev Glover's desk. Kev stood up. Then the two boys were eyeball-to-eyeball.

"Please everyone, please!" shouted Miss Bloor.

Nobody was listening, but they'd picked up on the tension between Matt and Kev, and the mantra now changed to "Scrap! scrap! scrap! scrap!"

The boys barged and shoved each other. A moment later, they collided with the low table in the middle of the room and fell straight on top of the model. Following a stunned silence, Miss Bloor came over to inspect the damage. All the buildings had been smashed to pieces. Visibly trembling, Miss Bloor picked up a roof section of one flattened building and it fell apart in her hand. Matt saw that her face was white. He didn't doubt that his own face had drained of all colour, too.

"Oh, no, no, no, no ..." Miss Bloor said in a whisper. "I don't know what Mr Warrilow ... Oh, dear, dear, dear ..."

13

Warrilow & Deakin

Miss Bloor had been unable to continue with the lesson. She sat at the front desk shuffling papers around and darting her eyes to the door at the slightest sound. Matt and Kev were back at their desks. Classmates kept their eyes down and pretended to read their textbooks.

The door burst open.

"Morning, class! Morning, Miss Bloor!"

Matt had never seen Warrilow looking so happy.

"I have splendid news," he gushed. The usual yellow-grey pallor of his haggard face had a rosier glow. "I've just come from the hospital, where I was holding a tiny new baby girl in my hands. I'm a grandfather at last!"

"Oh, that's wonderful," said Miss Bloor, but her voice was monotone. "Isn't it, class?"

There were some positive murmurs, mostly from the girls, but the overriding atmosphere was still one of doom. The ruined London street model was all Matt could think about. Warrilow stood at the front, beaming around the room. How could he not have seen the devastation? He even seemed to be looking directly at the model at one point, and Matt's heart felt close to rupturing. Warrilow was all smiles, and his twinkly gaze moved on to sweep around the class again.

"Mr Warrilow," said Miss Bloor. "I'm so happy for you and your family. But there is an ... incident to report."

Warrilow showed her the flat of his hand.

"Not now, Miss Bloor," he said. "I want everybody to join me in prayer."

Matt's thoughts were spinning.

Was it possible that Warrilow had seen the wrecked model, but was so happy that he didn't care?

"Put your hands together and close your eyes, please, everybody," he instructed. "Dear, Lord. We thank you this day for the safe arrival of Baby Belinda ..."

When Warrilow had finished and everybody had mumbled "amen", he hung his jacket on the back of his chair, sat at his desk and lit a cigarette. Miss Bloor stood beside him, her head still bowed and her lips moving, possibly in some private prayer of her own. Warrilow blew a long stream of smoke up towards the ceiling.

"All right, Miss Bloor. I trust that you recapped on last lesson adequately? So, class, who can tell me ..."

Miss Bloor leaned close to Warrilow and spoke softly into his ear. Warrilow's eyes widened. He looked at the model, then at Matt and Kev. He finished his cigarette in three long draws, making the tip glow bright orange. Matt had never seen anybody smoke so fast. Warrilow sucked in the last drag, stubbed the cigarette out in the ashtray on his desk, then blew big plumes of smoke from his nostrils. He stood up and walked over to the model. For a long time, he examined the damage.

"It weren't my fault, sir," said Kev Glover in a small voice. "It were Baxter. He pushed me, sir ..."

Matt was fuming, but Warrilow made no sign that he'd even heard Kev Glover. While smiling pleasantly and looking from Matt to Kev repeatedly, Warrilow took off his tie, folded it neatly and placed it on the board with the broken model. He undid the top button of his shirt and rolled his sleeves up.

"Mr Warrilow," said Miss Bloor, "I don't feel well. I wonder if I could – "

"Pull yourself together, Miss Bloor. I'll deal with this. Make yourself useful and clean the blackboard. All right,

Baxter, Glover – come out to the corridor with me for a moment and we'll have a little word."

Clutching a yellow envelope, Vonnie had just turned the corner of the corridor when she stopped at the sound of a gruff, menacing voice.

"... an utter danger to society. What in Heaven's name have you got to say for yourselves? No, don't speak. I was being rhetorical, not that either of you numbskulls would have the faintest inkling of what that means ..."

The door to Warrilow's class was at the end of the corridor. Vonnie saw Warrilow, Matt and Kev Glover standing outside, sandwiched between the wall on one side and the ranks of metal lockers on the other. She was only ten paces away, but none of them had seen her yet; she considered going away and coming back later.

Then Warrilow clapped Kev Glover around the head. The boy crashed into the lockers, yelled out and began to cry. Warrilow turned and gave Matt a blow to the head. It had such force behind it that Matt was knocked off his feet. He lay still for a second, then started to get up. Kev Glover whimpered and raised his hands as Warrilow approached him again.

"Please, sir. I'm sorry, sir. It were Baxter."

And it seemed that Warrilow was satisfied with Kev's cowering manner and tears.

Matt was on his feet now. His face was flushed and he looked stunned. Vonnie was impressed to see that he wasn't crying.

Warrilow grabbed him by the blazer lapels and pushed him into the wall.

Vonnie took a deep breath and marched forward.

"Mr Warrilow," she said.

Warrilow glared in her direction and released Matt.

"What? What are doing out of your class, girl?"

She raised the yellow envelope.

"I was told – "

"Told? Told? Told what? By whom?" He glanced at Matt and the other boy. "Right. That'll do for now, you two. Get back into class and think yourselves lucky you weren't sent to Mr Deakin."

Vonnie had heard that Mr Deakin kept a size 12 plimsoll for dealing out punishment, but she couldn't imagine a plimsoll across the backside being worse than what she'd just witnessed.

"Right," said Warrilow when he and Vonnie were alone. "Do not dare answer me back when I'm speaking."

"No, sir," she said, looking him in the face and half raising the yellow envelope again.

"I'll tell you when to speak."

"Yes, sir."

"I know who you are, girl. Rivers. Yvonne Rivers. Mr Schofield's form. You're a trouble-maker. Your mother ran away from your father when you were little, breaking the bonds of holy matrimony." He narrowed his eyes. "You don't even look like a proper girl. That short hair makes you look like a hooligan. You're an utter danger to society. Straight to Mr Deakin's office, please. Tell him you were out of your class at lesson time, swanning about the school and doing whatever you liked. Go on then. Off you go. I'll be checking with Mr Deakin later."

He went back into the classroom and closed the door.

Vonnie looked at the yellow envelope in her hand and wondered whether to knock on the door and try again.

"Everybody's staying back for detention tonight," came Warrilow's muffled voice.

Vonnie made her way up to Mr Deakin's office. The white-haired old man was already outside his office, fumbling with keys to lock the door. He jumped when he turned around to see Vonnie standing there. It was the first time she'd seen him up close. He had very hunched shoulders and looked incredibly old; he was actually a couple of inches shorter than Vonnie.

"What is it, missie?" said Deakin in his feeble voice.

Vonnie raised the yellow envelope.

"It's this, sir."

Deakin snatched the envelope from her.

"I've no time for riddles. It says 'Percy Warrilow' on the front. That's our *Mr* Warrilow."

"Yes, sir. I was told to give him it."

"No such phrase in the English language as 'give him it'. Give it to him."

"Yes. I was told to give it to him by my French teacher, Mrs Griffiths. She saw him on his way into school after he was at the hospital. His daughter had a baby. And so this is a card for Mr Warrilow that she got all of us in the French class to put our names on."

"Very well," said Deakin. "Why have you come to me?"

"Mr Warrilow was ... busy. He didn't understand. He thought I was skiving out of my lesson."

Deakin pulled a distasteful expression.

"You're not making any sense, girl."

"Mr Warrilow was telling some boys off in the corridor when I got there, sir. He was hitting them. Hitting them really hard."

Deakin sniffed and put the envelope inside his jacket.

"I'm sure he would have had a very good reason. I'll take care of the envelope. Look lively, then, missie. Back to your lesson. If I had it my way, you'd all be lined up in the playground and I'd have Mr Warrilow knocking some sense into every last one of you."

14

She's Leaving Home

Dusk was settling as Vonnie cycled along Grebble Street, the tyres of her racer hissing gently. The long rows of terraced houses all looked alike with their tiny, walled, front yards and their arched, gated entries. She didn't know what number Matt lived at, but she'd asked around and been told that it had an old cooker outside.

A group of young boys were playing football across the width of the road, and one of them was being called in by his mother. Other children sat on the low walls of the yards or ran in and out of the entries. Everybody paused and looked down the street as a Mr Whippy ice-cream van appeared, its jingly music playing. A man in a boiler-suit was working on the engine a Hillman Minx. Vonnie was good at recognising car makes, and Minxes were her favourite just because her favourite comic character was Minnie the Minx. The only other cars on the street were a Ford Escort, a Mini and a Morris Minor.

At number 48, the house with the cooker outside, she wheeled her racer into the front yard and leaned it against the wall. Her knocks on the door went unanswered.

She felt shaky and a bit sick. There were no lights on in the downstairs or upstairs windows. What was she going to do if nobody was in? She left her bike where it was and went to the gated entry, relieved to find it unlocked.

A cool breeze blew through the dusky foot-passage. On Vonnie's left, there was a washing-line strung against the brick wall, and a collection of men's long underpants billowed about like ghosts.

At the end of the passage, she opened the gate on the right, and then she was standing in Matt's narrow back yard. She felt suddenly vulnerable in the tight space with light flooding out from the windows. She could see people sitting inside and the flicker from a television in the corner closest to where she stood. The house dog-legged off down the yard with a kitchen and some outbuildings. She knew it was a kitchen because she could see a woman doing the washing-up at the sink.

Vonnie knocked on the back door.

It was opened by the woman, who wore a flowery apron and seemed pleasantly surprised to see Vonnie, though they'd never met.

"Hello, dear," she said.

"Does Matt Baxter live here?" said Vonnie.

"Yes, dear. Come in."

Vonnie recognised Matt's mother's voice as a diluted version of the voice she'd heard before on the phone.

"Is Matt all right?" said Vonnie as they stood in the narrow kitchen.

"He's upstairs in his room listening to records."

"Er, I mean was he all right when he came home from school earlier?"

The memory of Warrilow's violence resurfaced. It was compounded by the more immediate memory of Skinner raging at her for leaving her bedroom light on all day.

"Are *you* all right?" said Matt's mother. "You look as if you've – What's your name?"

"Vonnie ..."

Matt's mother swept Vonnie into her arms.

"There, there," she said. "It can't be that bad. Sit down in here a minute. I was about to take this pot of tea through to everybody, but sit down here at the table. That's it."

Seconds later, Matt's mother had put a cup of sweet tea in front of Vonnie and a big slice of apple pie.

Vonnie fought to hold back the tears.

91

"I'll call Matt down soon," said his mother. "You just take your time and tell me all about it if you want to."

Vonnie sipped at the tea and shook her head.

"I tried phoning earlier," she said.

"Oh, did you? The phone's on the blink this week. Do you want to tell me what's happened?"

Vonnie shook her head again.

The tea and the apple pie were delicious.

When she'd finished and was feeling calmer, she was shown into the living room and introduced to Matt's dad, his sister Jenny, and Jenny's boyfriend Mike.

"Hi, Vonnie, love your hair," said Jenny. "It's, like, really you. Perfect for your face. She's so pretty, isn't she, Mike?"

"Very," said Mike.

"You look like a junior Audrey Hepburn," said Dad. "I can see what Matt sees in you."

"Dad!" said Jenny playfully. "We don't even know if it's that kind of friendship."

"Another cup of tea, Vonnie?" said Matt's mother. "And another piece of apple pie?"

Vonnie smiled and shook her head.

She knew that if she tried to speak, she'd completely break down. Her chest and throat were swollen with emotion. She was stunned by how nice they were all being. It struck her like an epiphany that maybe this was how most people were. With nobody ever welcome at her own house, and with hardly ever going or being invited to other people's houses – maybe the life she was used to was even more extreme than she thought?

Matt's mother opened the door to the stairwell and called up. He must have come out to the landing, Vonnie thought, because she could hear him answering from quite close by. Then his mother said, "Vonnie's here."

There was a long pause.

"Down in a few minutes," Matt finally said.

But the few minutes became ten minutes.

Then fifteen minutes.

Matt's mother called up the stairs again, but he didn't answer. She went off to the kitchen and came back with two glasses of fizzy drink.

"Here you go, Vonnie. I'm sure you can manage some dandelion and burdock. There's a glass each. Top of the stairs, turn right and he's at the end of the landing."

The stairwell was dimly lit and smelled faintly musty, and the landing floorboards creaked.

Matt's bedroom door stood half open.

She knocked and waited.

"Oh ... hi, Vonnie," he said, appearing.

He took a drink from her, went back in and left her to follow. The light was off, but the curtains were open and the room was partly lit from the streetlamps.

"Sorry I came 'round like this," she said. "Your mum said the phone's not working. How was detention?"

Matt shrugged.

"Warrilow's an evil pig-dog," said Vonnie. "He should be made to live down a sewer. All alone. Or stuck down there with my pig-dog stepdad. Forever."

Matt smiled.

"Your family are really nice," said Vonnie.

She drank some of her dandelion and burdock.

Matt stood at the record player on the chest-of-drawers and operated the start switch. There was already a vinyl LP on the turntable. When the stylus arm lifted up and over the record, he reached out, arrested its movement and guided it down to a particular track.

Vonnie recognised the opening notes. It was the Beatles. 'Lucy In The Sky With Diamonds' from *Sgt. Pepper's Lonely Hearts Club Band*.

"Fab album," she said. "Is this your favourite track?"

"It's my sister's," he said.

He went to the window and looked out into the street. Vonnie joined him. As John Lennon's voice filled the room, she pictured herself "on a boat on a river" sailing away from everything under "marmalade skies". Then she snapped back to reality. She was here for a reason.

"Matt ..." she said.

"Yeah?" he said, still looking down into the street.

"I'm not going to school tomorrow."

"No? Why? You skiving off? I was thinking about skiving off myself."

"Good. Matt?"

"Yeah?"

"Please tell me that the shack's ready."

He looked at her.

"Uh ... yeah ... it's ready," he said.

Vonnie laughed with relief, moved closer to him and lay her head against his chest.

Matt backed away.

"When I say *ready* ..." he said.

But Vonnie laughed again.

"Don't worry if it's not *completely* ready. We have to go tonight. You said, didn't you? You said you wanted to get away, like me? To never go back to school. And now, after Warrilow ... And *I* don't ever want to go back home. My stepdad's a drunk and a bully and a selfish pig-dog. And Mam won't ever leave him. We really have to go to the shack tonight. Please say 'yes'. Please. I'll go home and get the curtains and a few other things and meet you at the end of Horsefair Road in half an hour – "

"Curtains?"

"Yeah. To divide it into two rooms." She nearly talked about how she was hoping to convince Mam to move in as well eventually, but she didn't want to give Matt anything else to think about. "Remember? We said about dividing it? Don't worry if you've not got the rod fixed up yet. It doesn't have to be divided straight away. I can help you with that bit anyway."

"Er, right," said Matt.

"The weather's good and everything," said Vonnie. "It's been dry since the weekend. It's not even cold. We'll need blankets though, and have you got a torch, and ..."

Matt was looking troubled.

"You still want to, don't you?" she said.

"Yeah ... but *tonight*?"

He moved away from the window, sat on the edge of his bed and stared at the carpet. Neither of them spoke. A few more tracks from the album played out. The Beatles went into the opening bars of 'She's Leaving Home'.

"You really want to go tonight?" said Matt.

"I can't go back there," she said. "I can't. Except to get my stuff. I've already left a note for Mam in my bedroom."

"A note?"

"To tell her I've gone. She won't see it till about six in the morning when she gets back from her night shift."

"Uh ... right. What about your stepdad?"

"He probably won't even realise I've gone," said Vonnie with a contemptuous snort. "He'll be too busy guzzling his beer and being a selfish pig-dog."

Matt laughed.

"Okay," he said. "End of Horsefair Road?"

"I'll be there in half an hour," said Vonnie. "At six."

15

Night Owls

When side 1 of the LP had ended, and the stylus arm had lifted away and clicked back into its start position, Matt headed downstairs.

He knew it was pointless looking for his torch. As far as he could remember, he'd tossed it under the wardrobe a year ago, its insides corroded from leaky batteries.

In the kitchen, he took his cord jacket from the back of the door and sat on the lino to pull his boots on.

"You going out?" said Mum.

"Just a walk 'round the block."

She was standing at the table making sandwiches for Dad's packed lunch. Matt went to the table and snatched a sandwich before she had fully wrapped them in the greaseproof paper.

"Oi," she said, though she was grinning. "I'll have to make another now. Vonnie's nice. Where does she live?"

"Dunno ... mmm ... cold meat and mustard."

He went to the pantry, lifted a box of matches from the top shelf and slipped them in his pocket.

"See you in a bit," he said as he opened the back door.

In the yard, he went to the outbuilding that adjoined the kitchen. The dank interior was piled high with clutter, but he spotted what he was looking for in a front corner of the quarry-tiled floor – a railway lantern that Dad had brought home some years back. Matt raised it by its handle and swept the cobwebs off. He shook it and smiled as he heard paraffin sloshing about in its base. There was an old donkey-jacket on a hook on the wall, too. It smelled of damp and mould, but he put it on over his cord jacket.

When he reached Horsefair Road, he could see Vonnie standing with her bike on the other side of the T-junction. From two hundred yards away, he thought that she had a small child sitting on the bike. As he approached, he saw that it was a big bundle balanced on the crossbar.

"Uh, the curtains ..." he said when he was beside her. "And blankets. What's in the bag?"

Vonnie frowned.

"Spare clothes, towel, toothbrush, toothpaste, soap," she said. "Toilet roll, torch, matches, candles, a knife, a book, some food, a flask of cocoa ... Where's *your* stuff?"

"Er, I'll be all right," he said.

"Sorry," said Vonnie. "You've probably got loads of stuff at the shack already."

The air was cool, dry, and smelled faintly of coal-fires. A breeze sent the yellow-brown leaves skittering about the road and pavement. There were no streetlamps on this side, and a narrow grass-verge gave directly onto the deep shadows at the edge of Blackthorn Woods. As they stood there, a motorbike and sidecar sputtered along Woodside Road, turned into Horsefair Road and sputtered its smoky way into the distance.

Vonnie had already taken out her torch and was shining its beam between the tree trunks.

"Just a sec," said Matt.

He squatted on the ground with the railway lantern. Its four sides each had a big round lens, and one side could be opened to light the wick. When it was lit, he put the matches back in his pocket and stood up.

"Great," said Vonnie. "Is it yours?"

"Sort of." He was surprised that the light being given off by the lantern was a deep orange. "I think it might be a signalman's warning lamp or something."

Vonnie nodded and waited for him to lead the way.

He held the lantern out in front of him and followed the familiar, well-trodden route through the trees.

The deeper they trekked into the wood, the less familiar it looked – bathed as it was in the orange glow from the lantern. The undergrowth rustled. Night birds called. The wind whispered in the semi-bare trees, and the dry carpet of leaves crackled beneath their feet.

"A few low branches coming up now," he said over his shoulder before ducking down.

"Thanks, Matt."

At another point, he held some spiky brambles aside for her, and after she'd wheeled her heavily-loaded bike through, he went ahead again.

All he could smell were paraffin fumes and the slightly scorched smell of the burning wick. Everything in his field of vision was washed in the orange light from the lantern.

It felt good leading the way, and having Vonnie with him as a companion. He was mostly able to push aside the uncomfortable truth of what waited at the end of the journey. For now, she believed in him and he believed in himself. Maybe they could just keep going? Trek all the way through the orange wood and out the other side? Over the hills and fields. Under marmalade skies. Until they simply found a shack in a moonlit valley. Where they could stay. And live off wild berries ...

Matt tripped over something, staggered forward, and stopped himself from falling.

"You okay?" said Vonnie.

He shone the lantern over the dried mud and leaves of the ground where he'd tripped. It was the two lengths of timber – the old fence posts he'd brought here himself to build the shack. Matt set the lantern down on the ground and picked up one of the posts.

"The shack's nowhere near ready, is it?" said Vonnie.

He carried the post to the top of the shallow bank and stood it upright, in position.

"This was going to be a corner," he said. "And that tree over there, and that one and that one – they're the other corners. It's a good spot."

"It's not even started?"

He lowered the post to the ground and sat down. Vonnie leaned her bike and bundle against a tree, grabbed her canvas bag and mounted the bank to sit beside him.

"I'm really sorry," he said. "I was going to build one. Honest. I *did* try .... We still could. There's a hammer and nails around here somewhere."

She didn't answer, but a moment later she was holding out cocoa for him in an enamelled tin camping-mug. It smelled delicious. He took it and laughed.

"You don't mess about, do you?" he said.

Vonnie sipped her own cocoa.

"I can't go home tonight," she said.

"No. I know. I could ask my Mum and Dad? They might let you stay at ours."

"No. I mean, thanks for thinking of that, and it would be really kind if they did, but that's not the point. We were supposed to be leaving our homes and leaving school."

"Yeah, it was only an idea about my house. There's loads of places we can stay in the woods anyway."

"Are there?"

"Er, well ... when I say *loads* ..."

They drank cocoa in silence for a while.

Although the lantern still cast its orange light all about, it had been left a little way off from where they sat, and Matt's eyes were adapting again. Except for the corner trees on the raised area, there was an absence of growth here, leaving a gap in the wood's canopy with only a few overhanging leafless boughs. The sky was the deepest indigo with a crescent moon and myriad stars.

Vonnie was looking up, too.

"Oh ..." she said as a large white bird sailed over. "Was that an owl?"

"Barn owl," said Matt. "Probably lives at the edge of the woods near Gallows Hill, or on Hill Farm."

"How do you know?"

"Nidge found a barn owl's nest in the old barn near Gallows Hill last year. I had to help him get an egg for his collection. I don't collect eggs myself though."

"Good. You helped him get a barn owl's egg though?"

"Yeah, well, I just kept watch while he climbed up inside the roof. We used to play there a lot, but the farmer came by on his tractor a few times and chased us off."

Vonnie gazed up into the night sky again and into the surrounding wood.

"I love it here. I wish there *was* a shack."

"We'll build it tomorrow," he said.

She smiled and touched his arm.

He leaned towards her and pushed his lips against hers clumsily. Vonnie sat back with a startled expression.

"What are you doing?"

"Uh, soz ..."

Vonnie touched his arm again briefly.

"No, *I'm* sorry, Matt. If I gave you the wrong idea ..."

Matt sniffed, shrugged, and drank the rest of his cocoa.

"It's okay if you don't want to kiss me," he said.

"It's not that," she said. "What I mean is, I don't know if I want to *be* kissed. By you or anybody."

He shuffled his feet and shrugged again.

"Is it because of my chin?" he said.

"What? Your *chin?* What's wrong with your chin?"

"You know, how it's a bit big and sticks out. You don't have to pretend it doesn't."

"Pretend? I don't know what you're talking about?"

Matt covered his chin with his hand.

Vonnie pulled his hand away and planted a kiss on his lips. Matt moved his lips against hers. After about ten seconds, Vonnie sat back.

"There's nothing wrong with your chin," she said.

100

Matt nodded.

"It suits you," she added. "It suits your face and there's nothing wrong with it. You're a good-looking lad. But I still don't know about the kissing. Okay?"

"Uh ... you're good-looking as well, but ... uh, nothing."

"What?"

"Nothing."

"No, really, Matt. *But* what?"

"All it is, is ... Can I ask you a favour?"

"Yeah. Anything."

"Thanks," he said. "Er, everything that's been going on tonight. You and me. In my bedroom. In the woods. The kissing. Especially the kissing. Don't tell Dawn ..."

16

Austin Cambridge

Don't tell Dawn? Vonnie was in Dawn Hagley's form class, and she'd known ever since the conker match in the playground that Matt fancied Dawn.

Now, Vonnie was even more confused about her own wants and needs. At school, so many girls went on and on about their first kiss – how romantic it had been, where it had happened, and so on. Vonnie's first kiss had been here and now. With Matt. And she wasn't sure how she felt about it, or even if she felt anything at all.

She wondered what it would be like to kiss a girl.

"I won't tell Dawn," she said.

Matt nodded and looked away.

Vonnie flicked the last few drops of cocoa from her cup and screwed the cup back onto the thermos flask.

"Is there *anywhere* we can stay?" she said.

"Er, maybe. There's an old car not far away. Been there for yonks. Still got doors and windows and seats."

Vonnie stood up.

"Let's go," she said.

Matt handed her his cocoa mug and trod down the shallow bank to retrieve the railway lantern.

After a five-minute trek, they reached the edge of the woods near Shady Lane. Whatever accident had led to the car's abandonment, its nearside front wheel had made it over the ditch and its offside front wheel was wedged in the ditch. Both rear wheels were still on the verge. Matt smiled at the familiarity of the bull-nosed design, its prominent headlamps and the faded grey of its bodywork.

MARMALADE SKIES / GUS GRESHAM

"The ditch is full of stingers," he told Vonnie. "So we use the car as a bridge."

"What, you climb over the top of it?"

"No. Look." He opened the front passenger-door, where the seat was missing. "You go in this way, then out the back door on the other side. And that's it. You're over the ditch. Or when you're coming into the woods, you come in the back door and out this door."

"It's an Austin Cambridge," said Vonnie.

"Yeah. I think it's a 1954."

Vonnie slung her bag, her blankets and the curtains into the back, then climbed in herself. She stretched her legs forward in the ample space left by the missing front seat. It was dusty and cobwebby inside, and smelled of perished leather, but it was dry and comfortable.

"It's pretty good," she said.

"Yeah ..." he said. "You can have the back seat if you like. Or the driver's seat. Your choice."

She climbed out of the other rear door and made her way through the weeds and bushes on the grassy verge, to the edge of Shady Lane. Matt set the railway lantern on the bonnet of the car and followed her.

"Does much traffic go along here?" she said.

"Not really. The odd car on its way to or from one of the villages maybe. We can't see much now, but it's just farm land on the other side of the hedgerow across the road."

As they stood there, a little black shape flitted in and out of view above their heads, followed by another.

"Bats," said Matt. "We'll see more if we keep looking."

"Really? They're so quick – oh, another. They're so quick I can't see what they are. How do you know it's bats?"

"I've seen loads before," he said. "On the way out of the woods at the end of Horsefair Road. At dusk. You know, when it's just getting dark."

There was a low rumble that got louder. Headlamps swept into the lane, lighting up the hedgerow opposite and

MARMALADE SKIES / GUS GRESHAM

the verge where Matt and Vonnie stood. They squatted among the tall weeds. A moment later, a lorry rumbled past, trailing exhaust fumes. The growl of its engine and the glow of the tail-lights faded away along the lane.

Without a word, Matt and Vonnie went back to the car. Matt operated the thumb-wheel of the lantern and turned the wick down until it went out. He left the lantern on the bonnet. And by the light of Vonnie's torch, they settled themselves in the Austin Cambridge.

"You sure you're okay about me being in the driver's seat?" he said.

Vonnie laughed.

"I really like it in the back," she said. "There's loads of room. Do you want some more cocoa?"

"Okay."

When she'd poured fresh cocoa for both of them, she took out her book and opened it at the familiar place.

"What's that?" he said.

"It's a collection of Slavic folk tales. I've only read one."

"Right," said Matt. "You going to read it out then?"

"Bit early for a bedtime story?"

"Yeah, I was only joking anyway."

Vonnie smiled and began to read aloud from a random place halfway through:

... Agata turned from the dead ashes of the mystic's funeral pyre, and made her way down the mountain. She set about travelling the land again. Each evening, she ate roots and berries by her fire, then slept under the great mystery of the whirling cosmos ...

"I'm sorry," she said, closing the book. "I don't think I can carry on." She couldn't explain her feelings to Matt, or even to herself very well, but it was as if the story were only for her, too personal to share with anybody.

"It sounded really good," he said.

"Sorry. I'm not in the mood."

Vonnie put the book back in her bag and took out a little black transistor-radio. She switched it on and set it down on the floor at the front. Joe Cocker was part way through 'Cry Me A River'.

Ten yards behind the Austin Cambridge, and on the slightly higher ground, there was the occasional rise and fall of an engine note and the sweep of headlamps.

The torch batteries had worn down and were almost dead when she turned it off. The crescent moon sailed over the woods, with a very bright star close by and masses of stars everywhere else. It was surprising to Vonnie how much light was cast. She could see a little way into the woods and a little way along Shady Lane in each direction if she craned her head.

The radio played on with 'Black Magic Woman' by Santana and 'Ride A White Swan' by T. Rex.

As it grew colder, she wrapped herself in a blanket and offered the other to Matt.

"I'm not really cold," he said.

"You're shivering," said Vonnie.

"They're your blankets though."

Vonnie pushed the blanket over to him and unfolded the dark-green velvety drapes.

"We'll use these as well," she said.

"Okay," he said. "We can swap seats anytime you like."

"I'm fine here," she said. "Do *you* want to swap?"

"No. I prefer it here. But I don't want to be greedy and keep the best seat."

"How is it the best seat?"

"It's the driver's seat," said Matt. "It's got the steering wheel and the gearstick and the dashboard."

Vonnie stopped herself from laughing.

"Well, that's all really groovy and everything," she said, "but it's not as if you can drive it anywhere."

"No. I know. It's still the best seat though."

He pushed the clutch pedal in with his foot and started shifting the gear stick into different positions.

"Has your dad got a car?" said Vonnie.

"No. Has yours?"

"Stepdad. He's got a Zodiac."

"Yeah, they're pretty nifty."

He changed gear again and grappled with the steering wheel, pulling it about to the left and the right.

"Just ... whatever you do," said Vonnie, "please don't start making *brrm-brrm* noises."

He laughed.

"I like you. You're funny."

"I like you too, Matt."

Vonnie stretched out into a lying position on the back seat and made herself comfortable under her blanket and curtain. The radio battery was running low as David Bowie sang about coming face to face with the man who sold the world. From Vonnie's position, she could see a section of night sky. The moon was behind her somewhere, but out over the farmland on the opposite side of Shady Lane she made out a wide band of faint light among the brighter stars and wondered if it was an arm of the Milky Way.

Her last thoughts, as her eyelids drooped, were of Agata sleeping under the great mystery of the whirling cosmos.

17

Wise Women

She was woken by a policeman shining a torch in her face.

As she roused herself, another policeman opened the driver's door and Matt all but fell out of the car.

"Come on then, Jackie Stewart," said the officer at Matt's door.

"Eh up," said the first officer as he opened Vonnie's door. "It's a girl in the back after all. I thought it was a bit funny. We were looking for a girl and a boy, and I thought we'd found two boys, but it's a girl in the back with a boy's haircut. Who are you supposed to be then, darling? I'll tell you what, Bert – forget Jackie Stewart. I think we've got ourselves Bonnie and Clyde."

"Nah," said the other, shining the beam of his torch over Matt's tousled hair and startled face. "More like Dick Dastardly and Penelope Pitstop."

The officers quickly worked out the safest route from inside the car, avoiding the abundant nettles in the ditch. And still half asleep, Vonnie found herself and Matt being chaperoned to the waiting panda car – a Ford Anglia with the usual two-tone white and pale-blue paintwork.

"My things ... my bike ..." she said.

With Matt and Vonnie seated in the back, one of the officers collected Vonnie's things. Her bike ended up sticking out of the boot, the lid secured with rope.

"Er, there's a railway lantern on the bonnet as well," said Matt. "It's my dad's. Sorry ..."

The officer went back for the lantern, and a minute later the panda car was zooming along Shady Lane.

"Right, Matthew Baxter and Yvonne Rivers," said the officer in the front passenger-seat, the one who'd retrieved their belongings, "your parents are worried sick."

It was still dark outside, and Vonnie saw that the hands of the dashboard clock showed just before five.

The car stopped at Matt's house first. One of the officers took him inside, was back in about three minutes, and then Vonnie was taken home.

A milk float was already trundling along the street.

"Six hours!" said Mam when the police had left. "Six hours of wondering if you were dead or alive."

"I left a note," said Vonnie.

"So what did you think?" said Mam. "That I'd read the note and think you'd be all right by yourself? That you wouldn't get picked up by a lunatic or a sex maniac?"

"I've had no sleep yet!" said Skinner. "The alarm'll be going off in a couple of hours."

"Poor Bill's been awake all night," said Mam. "I have as well, but that's different. I would have been working. They came and got me from the hospital, the police. Bill realised you'd disappeared and found your note."

"I'm sorry," said Vonnie.

"Not good enough," said Skinner. "I've got to go to work with hardly any sleep. Are my sandwiches made?"

Because he was still glaring at Vonnie, it took a second before Mam realised that he was speaking to her.

"Yes, they're ready," she said. "Did them before I went to work. New rules from now on, Vonnie. No going out after dark. No going out without checking with me or Bill first. No more playing in the woods – "

"Homework straight after school," said Skinner. "Wash the dishes every night. No more knocking around with that Grebble Street kid, whoever he is. Or any of his mates. Bed at eight o' clock. No pocket money for a month. No

Christmas presents. And I wouldn't hold your hopes out for any birthday presents in January either."

"Bill ..." said Mam. "I don't know if – "

"I'm going to bed," he said. 'You coming?"

"I ... might have a cup of tea first," said Mam.

"Don't make any noise when you come up then. Use the downstairs toilet and don't pull the chain. Don't put the light on when you come in the room. When you come up the stairs, go really slow. Test each stair before you put your full weight on it. If it makes the slightest creak – "

"Bill – "

"Shut up when I'm talking, you. If there's the slightest creak, move your foot to a different stair. Go really slow. Both of you. It doesn't matter if it takes you half an hour to get upstairs. Just don't make any noise."

He turned in the hall doorway.

"As for you," he said to Vonnie, "one more trick like this and you'll be sent straight to borstal. I'll see to that."

Vonnie waited until she heard the bedroom door close upstairs and said, "I don't want to go to borstal."

"You won't be going to borstal," said Mam. "But please don't ever do anything like that again."

Mam started crying again and Vonnie hugged her.

"I won't. I'm really sorry."

... One day, Agata saw her reflection in a pool, and noticed that her skin was lined. Nobody would engage her as a trade apprentice now. In fact, she'd wasted half her life trying to honour her father's memory. Nowhere in the land had she met another female who worked a trade. But what choices did she have? Would anybody want to marry her now? Would anybody even take her on as a labourer?

Was it too late for her?

If she could just solve the riddle of her sign, she might know what to do, might still find happiness.

109

Then, at the spring equinox, she overheard some woodcutters talking about a wise old woman. It was said that the woman knew the answer to every problem. Agata approached the woodcutters.

When they'd taken turns kicking her, they said that the wise woman lived yonder, on an island in the middle of a lake. The waters were infested with deadly creatures, but the woodcutters guided Agata to the edge of the lake, where they built her a crude raft. She sailed to the island and found the wise old woman sitting before a fire, cooking a meal.

Agata was invited to eat, and such a meal of fish, wild mushrooms and root vegetables she hadn't tasted for many a year.

"You didn't kick me," she said.

"No," said the old woman. "Not everybody kicks you, do they?"

Agata thought about this. Many, many people had kicked her in her life – so many, she admitted, that it truly seemed as if the many were all ...

The next afternoon at school, Vonnie fell apart in her maths lesson. She'd been stifling the tears all day. Word had got around about "the runaways", and she was teased relentlessly. She couldn't bear the thought of living with Skinner any longer. But she didn't want to hurt Mam either, and Mam was on Skinner's side. Obviously.

Poor Bill's been awake all night.

Mr Harris, Vonnie's maths teacher, didn't know what to do with her. He left the room for ten minutes and came back with Vonnie's form teacher, Mr Schofield, who didn't know what to do either. After some thought, Mr Schofield took Vonnie to what was known as the Sick Room.

The Sick Room had no windows. It smelled of dust and damp. The walls were lined with bookcases filled with ancient books. Vonnie was sitting in one of four wingback armchairs that looked like museum pieces. She wondered with a twisted smile whether this was where Blackthorn Modern's retired teachers came to die. One thing was for certain, anybody who was genuinely sick would feel a lot worse if they spent much time in here.

Vonnie had been told to stay in the Sick Room for "a while", but nothing had been said about how long "a while" was, or what she was expected to do next.

So she just waited, content to be alone and have the chance to pull herself together a bit, lost in thought.

> ... *Agata told her story to the wise woman. Told of how she'd often thrown the sign away or burned it, but always fell into a deep swoon and awoke with it back around her neck. Of how the mystic had tried to help her, and of how – even though the words had been changed to read, DON'T KICK ME – wherever she went, many people still kicked her.*
>
> *And she told of how she worried that it was too late to be taken on as a trade apprentice, or to marry and have children.*
>
> *"Are they the only two choices?" said the woman.*
> *"I don't understand."*
> *"Do you believe your only choices are the work of the world, or raising a family? Not some other path?"*
> *"What path?"*

After fifteen minutes or so, there was a gentle knock at the door of the Sick Room. It slowly opened. The woman who came in had a kind face and shoulder-length reddish hair.

"Hello, Yvonne," she said, sitting in the nearest chair.

"Oh, Miss Kovacs ... Er, I'll definitely bring my history homework in on Friday."

Miss Kovacs shook her head.

"That's not why I'm here. And, please, for now I want you to call me Magda. Or Maggie."

Vonnie told the whole story about how she'd met Matt at the woods, spent the night in the Austin Cambridge and been taken home by the police.

Magda Kovacs listened patiently and smiled in all the right places. Then she said:

"I understand, Yvonne. Or is it Vonnie? You like to be called Vonnie, don't you? I already know the story of what happened last night. All the staff know. The police came to the school earlier. But I want to understand the reason *why* this happened. And yes, all right, I can see that you may not want to talk about it. Don't worry. You're not in trouble. So ... Perhaps I understand more than you might think. You've been in my history group all these months. I've watched you. Seen ... little things in you. Heard little things you say. Little slips of the tongue. I don't mean to be nosey or putting you under a microscope. But myself, in Hungary, I had a difficult childhood and then many years later, living in London, I had a very difficult marriage. And now ... I am free from my violent husband. I am well. I *see* things. I can read things in people's hearts and minds that they may not even understand themselves, or things that they believe to be secrets ... but still I sometimes see those things ... Vonnie, do you have problems at home? Your parents? Your father?"

"Stepfather."

"Ah."

"I mean, he's my stepfather, not my father. That's what I meant. I wasn't saying anything was wrong with him."

"Hm-hm," said Magda. "So he's a very kind man?"

"What? No, I ..."

There was another knock at the door.

"Come in," said Magda.

One of the dinner-ladies entered, set down a tray and left again. There were cups and saucers, a teapot, a milk jug, a sugar bowl, and chocolate digestives on a plate.

The dinner-lady smiled pleasantly at Vonnie and left.

112

"You see," said Magda. "No hurry. No lessons to get back to. Just the two of us drinking tea and chatting."

Vonnie could hardly believe what was happening. She accepted the cup of tea that Miss Kovacs had stirred two heaped spoons of sugar into.

Then it started getting stranger.

"I think perhaps your stepfather is mean to you?" said Magda. "Very strict. Shouts a lot. Angry. Suspicious. Mean to your mother, too, I expect."

Vonnie half shook her head, lowered her eyes.

"Yes, I know, Vonnie. It's very difficult to live in a house with somebody like that."

"I, er ... I didn't say you were right."

"So I'm wrong? Your life at home is a rose garden?"

Vonnie stared at the carpet.

"And your mother?" said Magda. "She would like to leave him but she is terrified of him?"

"How do you ...? I don't understand, Miss Kovacs."

"You may understand when you're older. People who have bad experiences can often see those experiences in others. Listen. I am new at Blackthorn since the summer. In London, I was helped by an extraordinary woman. Erin Pizzey. She is trying to set something up in London. A special refuge. A safe place for women whose husbands have treated them badly. Women with children, too. I stayed with her for a time. Last winter. She made me welcome in her house. Fortunately, I did not have any children to worry about. Just myself."

Magda laid a hand on Vonnie's arm.

"Some men are simply monsters."

Vonnie wanted to tell Miss Kovacs everything about Skinner, but she was afraid. Skinner was so suspicious. He seemed to have an almost supernatural way of reading what was in her thoughts. She worried that she might give herself away at home if she said too much now. That if she confided in somebody, he would just *know*.

"You see," said Magda, "there is nothing to help women who are trapped in marriages with dangerous, abusive men. No adequate law. Society ... I believe that maybe women are the only ones who can truly help women."

Vonnie frowned and joined her hands in her lap.

"Er, he's always angry and mean," she said. "And I think he probably hits Mam sometimes. But even if some of the things about my stepdad were true ... I mean, *if* ..."

Magda glanced towards the door, then took out a pen and notebook. She scribbled something on a page, tore the page out and placed it in Vonnie's hand.

"I could probably be in a lot of trouble with Mr Deakin and the school authorities, but some matters in life are more important than worrying over your job. That's my address in Blackthorn. I live with two other women. Friends. What I am saying to you, Vonnie, is do not ever do anything dangerous again, like running away into the woods at night, or running away anywhere. Please. Not without your mother anyway. But if you are in serious need of help, come and find me. I'll do what I can."

"Er, thanks. I don't know what to say."

Magda picked up the plate from the table and pushed it towards Vonnie.

"Have a biscuit?" she said.

18

Party Seven

Matt didn't know that the police had visited the school, but just before lunchbreak he was sent to Mr Deakin's office. A session with the size 12 plimsoll left him with a sore backside for the rest of the day.

At home later in the afternoon – following some energetic gang business of stoning the windows derelict factories on Camber Street – he went straight up to his room. Even though it was colder today, he pulled open the sash-window and leaned on the sill to watch the street.

A group of young kids were chasing one another and playing some kind of war game with plastic guns and rifles. Nineteen-year-old Johnny Lynch was tinkering with the engine of his motorbike. It was an A65 Lightning, which he'd bought brand-new only a year ago. Matt knew from chatting to Johnny before that the bike had a 650 cc engine. He thought about going across the street to chat again now, but in the next minute Johnny had gathered up his tools and gone inside.

As Matt carried on watching from the window, the rag-and-bone man came along, leading his old horse and cart down the middle of the road.

"Aaanny rag-bone," he called out. "Raaag bone."

Charlie Smith dragged an ancient sewing-machine out from his entry and dragged it to the edge of the pavement. The rag-and-bone man looked it over, gave Charlie a few coins, then hoisted it aboard the cart. He halted the horse again outside Matt's house to consider the old cooker in the front yard. He must have thought it was too heavy or too much trouble though, because he quickly moved on.

"*Aaanny rag-bone.*"

Suddenly, Jenny was in Matt's bedroom doorway. She told him off over the night in the woods and for upsetting Mum and Dad. Matt looked at the floor and said nothing.

Eventually, he went downstairs.

In the kitchen, Mum was still in a bad mood. Matt couldn't understand it. They'd yelled at him at five o'clock this morning. And he'd had the whack from Deakin. What more did anybody want from him?

He sat on his usual stool, tilted it back against the wall on two legs, and picked absently at the blue Fablon that was coming away from the seat in places.

"Can I have a glass of Nesquik?"

"Have what you want," said Mum. "You know where everything is."

"Can you make it, though? You do it better than me."

She sighed and went to the pantry, poured milk into a glass and stood it on the draining board. Matt watched as she added a tablespoon of pink powder from the carton and whisked it into the milk with a fork.

"I don't know how I've got through the day," she said. "Good job I'm on earlies at the factory and came home at two. Tired to death, I've been. After all the palaver."

"I can't believe you're still going on about it," said Matt. "And I don't know how the fuzz even found us."

"I told you. Half past four this morning, just when we were picturing you dead in a ditch somewhere, your dad remembered you borrowed a hammer a month ago. Said you were building a shack in the woods near Shady Lane."

She put the glass of Nesquik in front of him.

"I was going to have chocolate flavour."

"Bloody well do it yourself next time then," she snapped.

"Bloody will do. Don't worry."

"Watch your language."

116

"Yeah, I will if everybody shuts up about last night. I've been told off enough."

"I'd make yourself scarce before your dad gets in if I was you. Somebody from the *Herald* rang here earlier. Wanted to speak to him. Wouldn't say nothing to me but I said they could find him at the railway yards. That'll be the next thing: your name in the paper."

"What? Why did you tell 'em where to find him?"

"Because I didn't want them coming to the house."

"Well I've had enough! I had the whack from Deakin today an' all. Size 12 plimmy."

"Did you?" said Mum. She pursed her lips. "I don't agree with hitting children. Not at home or school. Should be a law against it, there should. Are you all right?"

"Yeah. Course I am."

He wondered what she'd say if he told her about yesterday's punishment from Warrilow.

Mum washed some potatoes and started peeling them on the draining-board. Matt got the chocolate-flavoured Nesquik from the pantry and added a spoon of it to the glass. He prised the lid off the treacle tin and stirred some of that in, too. Then he took the jar of lemon curd from a shelf and added a big dollop to the mixture.

"You'd better make sure you drink that now," said Mum.

"Bloody will do. Don't worry."

The concoction was nauseating, but with perseverance he managed to get it down. He was wondering whether to spoon the sludge from the bottom of the glass when the back door opened and Dad walked in.

"You're early," said Mum.

"Oh, crap," said Matt. "Soz about the reporters, Dad. Am I in trouble?"

"Let's hear the worst then, Ron," said Mum. "What did the *Herald* have to say?"

"Didn't they tell you?"

"No. They didn't say a word."

117

"Right," said Dad. "That'll be because it's always just my name on the coupon then."

"Coupon?"

Dad let out an enormous guffawing laugh.

"We've only gone and won Where's The bloody Ball! Five hundred smackers!"

He ran to Mum and planted a big kiss on her lips. He lifted her off her feet and spun her around.

"What going on?" said Jenny, coming through from the living-room.

Matt jumped off his stool and ran around whooping.

"Ronnie!" said Mum. "It can't be true. Five hundred?"

"Five hundred smackers!" said Dad. "We're rich!"

"We've won Where's The Ball!" Matt told Jenny.

They laughed and hugged each other.

Then the whole family were jumping up and down, laughing and shouting and running all over the house. They ran out to the back yard and skipped about in the weeds. They ran up the entry and out to the street.

"You all look very happy," said Mr Patel. He was watering the potted plants that sat in a line along his front-yard wall.

"Too right, Raj," said Dad. "We've only gone and won Where's The bloody Ball!"

"Many congratulations."

"Don't worry. There'll be a few Party Sevens coming your way next week. Er ... do you drink beer?"

"I do. Very kind of you, Ron."

Dad led everyone back down the entry.

In the kitchen, he took out his wallet.

"Right," he said. "Talking of Party Sevens, you can nip to the offie, Matt. Do a note, will you, Dot? Jenny, go with him. He'll never carry it all by himself."

"Have you got the money already?" said Mum.

"It's a cheque. It'll take a week to clear. We're having a little party tonight, though. I've got about five bob ..."

Mum found her purse and checked its compartments.

"I've only got a few shillings for groceries. Mind you, I've got the stamps on the Christmas Club savings card from Lovell's. We could cash it in."

"Nice one, Dot," said Dad. "Matt, Jenny, go to Lovell's first and cash the Christmas stamps in. Let's do the note for the offie: six Barley Wines for you Dot – "

"I'll never drink all that in one night."

"Get 'em anyway. What's that drink you like, Jen?"

"Babycham."

"Get some Babychams for Jenny. Pop for Matt. He can have a glass of Watneys as well, as long as he don't tell no-one. Get a Party Seven – no, get two Party Sevens. Load of crisps, some salted peanuts, and get me another packet of Park Drives."

"*Two* Party Sevens?" said Mum. "They hold seven pints each, don't they? You won't drink all that tonight. Why not just get a couple of Party Fours?"

"Nah, get the Party Sevens. They're the best. The other one'll keep for Christmas."

Half an hour later, Matt watched excitedly as Dad struggled with a penknife, a screwdriver, pliers and a corkscrew at the draining-board, trying to open one of the huge cans of beer. Standard tin-openers wouldn't work because the ridge of the can was too high.

"I need a hammer," said Dad.

"Hold on, Ronnie," said Mum, rummaging through the cutlery drawer. "It's in here somewhere – "

"What's that?" said Dad.

"Ah, here we go. The proper thingamajig."

Dad took the flat metal implement from her and punctured the top face of the can with a neat triangular hole at each side. He grappled with the enormous can and filled two glass.

"Take your time with yours, Matt," he said.

Matt gulped at the frothy beer.

Jenny had already flipped the top off a Babycham and started quaffing it straight from the bottle.

"Thanks, Dad," she said. "This is far out."

"We could go and sit in the Best Room," said Mum. "That might be nice."

"Nah," said Dad. "It's party time. I always feel as if I'm waiting to be embalmed in there. Tell you what – we'll stick the gramophone on really loud and leave the door open while we sit in the living room. You can be the DJ, Matt. Let's start off with some Elvis, followed by Andy Williams for your mum, Led Zeppelin or whatever for you, then some Jimi Hendrix for Jenny."

"Can I phone Jack and tell him," said Mum.

"Course you can; tell him to come over for a drink."

"I wish Mike was here," said Jenny.

"Tell him to come and stay at the weekend," said Dad.

He was already a good way into the Party Seven by the time Jimi Hendrix was belting out 'Purple Haze'. Matt was allowed another half glass of beer, too.

"We're in for a great Christmas," said Dad. "Jenny, you're getting fifty quid to start you off in London if you're still determined to move there in the new year; Matt's getting a new bike."

"Wow!" said Jenny. "You're the best."

"Yeah," said Matt.

"A big holiday next summer as well," said Dad.

"I'd like to redecorate this living room," said Mum.

"Course we can. And let's order the biggest Christmas turkey the shop can get."

19

Creatures In The Snow

"Never trust nobody," said Skinner, topping up his beer glass from a fresh bottle of Double Diamond. "Never trust nobody. That's my motto now."

It had to be the worst Christmas that Vonnie could remember – not because of the new rules, which Mam had somehow managed to slacken, but because of the effect of what had happened to Skinner at work yesterday. He'd angrily retold the story over and over, and had been fretting about it all through Christmas dinner. Now, with each bottle of beer he guzzled, as he sat with his legs spread, taking up the whole of the sofa, his mood grew darker and more twisted.

"It was really disgusting of them," said Mam from the armchair, where she nursed a glass of sherry.

Skinner leaned forward and spoke loudly to Vonnie.

"Best advice I can give you, that is," he said. "Never trust nobody. The world's rotten, and everyone in it."

"Er ... okay," she said, looking up from reading a Minnie the Minx episode in her new Beano annual.

She was sitting on the carpet by the hearth.

"And don't hog that fire," said Skinner. "You're blocking all the heat for everybody else."

The fire had almost burnt down to nothing, so there wasn't much heat to block. It was always cold in the house in winter because Skinner was too stingy to have good fires. Vonnie shuffled along, closer to the twinkling tree. She glanced out at the snow falling in the back garden, then she stared into the dying embers of the fire and imagined it was the mystic's funeral pyre from the Slavic folk tale. Her best present had been the heavy-knit purple jumper that she was wearing now. She'd pointed it out to Mam when they'd been in town together one Saturday, browsing the department stores, which had all seemed to be playing 'White Christmas' by Bing Crosby.

During recent weeks at school, she knew that Matt had been avoiding her. She'd hoped that they might at least have talked about the night in the woods.

Heavy snow had fallen all over Blackthorn. It was beautiful, but it seemed it would never stop. By now, the pavements were impacted with snow and ice, and thick grey sludge lined the roadsides – sloppy and dirty in the daytime, razor-sharp and architectural when temperatures dropped in the evenings.

"I know who was behind it," said Skinner. "That long-haired git with the 'tache."

"Still ..." said Mam. "It wasn't your fault if the drawing was wrong."

"You're not listening. The drawing was right. I *told* you. It had a stain on it, see. I couldn't make out the thread dimension. It looked like three-eighths Whitworth. But it was five-eighths. And the stain ... The whole batch of a thousand bolts – useless! It grieves me, it does. The waste. And making a balls-up like that. Chargehand said I should have realised the thread gauge didn't match the hex-head size. But I thought it was a *special*. I ended up looking like an idiot. Never make mistakes, me. Never!"

"That's right," said Mam.

Skinner took a long swallow of beer.

"Can we switch over for the Christmas special of *Top Of The Pops*?" said Vonnie. "It's starting any minute."

"No," said Skinner. "Load of screaming rubbish. I'm watching *this* anyway."

On the little black-and-white telly in the corner of the room, an Edward G Robinson film played to itself.

122

"If you're bored, do that jigsaw puzzle we got you. Better still, go and shovel the snow off the front path again."

"Bill," said Mam. "Not on Christmas Day. Please."

"Anyway," said Vonnie. "There's not much I really like in the charts at the minute. Except for 'Ride A White Swan'. They won't put that on. It'll be Clive Dunn with 'Grandad'. Or, worse still, 'I Hear You Knocking'."

"Oh, I really like that song," said Mam. "I didn't know it was Clive Dunn as well, though."

"No, it's not. It's Dave Edmunds. It's really annoying."

"I like it. Everyone's been singing it on the ward."

Vonnie pulled a face and went back to the Beano annual.

"Don't keep going on about work," said Skinner.

"Sorry," said Mam.

"You're bringing it all back to me again. Shock of my life, it was, when I walked up the shop-floor and saw it there. I couldn't even work in the Capstan bay till the afternoon."

"You told us," said Mam.

"Put me on a poxy little lathe at the back."

"You told us."

"I know I told you! Go steady with that sherry if you're gonna start being lippy. The idiots ... Melting everywhere. Heat from the machines, see. Even when they'd got rid of it, it took the labourers all morning to swab the bay out."

Skinner stood up.

"It was *him*. I know it was. That long-haired git with the 'tache. He's been on nights this month. It had to be the night shift that built it. No other way."

Vonnie smiled secretly to herself.

Skinner hadn't gone into exact details in front of her. All she supposedly knew was that the blokes at the factory had made fun of him by building an enormous snowman in his machine bay. It had been so big that it had blocked the entrance. But as Vonnie had lain awake late last night, she'd heard the full story being ranted at Mam downstairs. Apparently, the snowman had had some of the duff bolts for eyes and nose, and had worn a tall conical hat with a capital D on it – a dunce's hat.

"Try to live a peaceful life ..." said Skinner.

"That's right," said Mam.

"I'm going to the bog," he said. "Don't nobody touch that telly. Right?"

He left the room and then there was the sound of the toilet door closing across the hall.

"That jumper looks lovely on you, Vonnie," said Mam.

"Thanks. I really love it."

"You're ... a good girl ..."

Vonnie realised that Mam was crying. She went to the armchair, sat on the arm and gave Mam a hug.

"I'm all right, I'm all right," said Mam, sniffing back the tears. "Go back over there. He'll – "

"You're not all right, Mam. *We're* not all right. We need to get away from him."

"Mm ... maybe in a few years ... Anyway, I'm upset about something else as well. A chap who came onto the ward last week. He fell off a roof. Back and head injuries. He's ever so friendly. You know, a lot of patients moan and complain, but Freddie's ever so brave. Always a smile. I really hope he recovers."

"Yeah, I hope so too," said Vonnie. "But we need to leave Skinner." She'd said nothing about Magda Kovacs yet. When the toilet flushed across the hall, she spoke quickly. "There's a teacher at school. She was really kind to me when I was upset, after the night in the woods. She said she might be able to help us. I ... And there's this wise woman in London who's trying to – "

"London? Wise woman? Who's this teacher of yours? I'll go to the school and give her a good talking to. Vonnie, our personal business is nothing to do with anybody else – "

"I know where he lives," said Skinner, appearing in the doorway. "I could ... What are *you* two plotting?"

"Nothing," said Mam.

"Something."

"No. Honestly. Vonnie was just saying thanks again for her jumper. Go and sit back over there, Vonnie."

"I could go 'round there now," said Skinner. "Lives on Hawker Street. That'd shake him up. If I knock on his door Christmas Day and have it out with him."

"Oh, Bill. I don't know if that's a good idea."

"What, you think I wouldn't?"

"No, I – "

"I'll go all right," said Skinner. He marched out to the hall and Vonnie heard the front door open.

"Bill," called Mam.

The front door closed and he came back to the living room. He stood with his hands on his hips.

"Oh, right! You don't want me to go then?"

"Not really," said Mam.

"I'll go. I will."

"I wish you wouldn't," said Mam.

"What? I'm going. Don't know the house number, but I know he's a got a Ford Capri. Oh, yeah, I'll go 'round, all right. He'll be all nice and cosy and I'll batter on his door, and when he answers, I'll say, 'Think you're clever, don't you?' And he'll say, all innocent like, 'I don't know what you're on about, mate'. And I'll say, 'Merry Christmas', and smack him one. Then ram my boot into his Capri."

"Bill, please ..."

He stamped back out to the hall.

"I'm going now," he called.

Mam tossed off the rest of her sherry and went to where the drink bottles were arranged on the sideboard.

There was the sound of the front door being opened again, and the sound of the knob being rattled.

"I said I'm going now!" called Skinner.

Mam poured another sherry, then sipped at it while she leaned back against the sideboard. Skinner stalked into the room again. He strutted about the carpet in tight circles, sweat on his brow, exuding darkness. His hairy forearms were on show, the sleeves of his plaid shirt rolled up.

"I'm having him," he said, clenching his fists. "Them houses are straight on the pavement. I'll have him right on his doorstep. Like this. Grab him with my left, see. Then *bosh!* with the right. *Bosh!* you scabby git. Punch his lights out. 'Try to make me look an idiot?' *Bosh! bosh!*"

"Charming," said Vonnie quietly.

"What? What did you say?"

"Nothing."

"Barmy?" said Skinner. "Sounded like you said *barmy.*"

"Charming," said Mam. "She said charming. And she's right. Come on, Bill. Please. It's Christmas Day."

Skinner stood over Vonnie, scowling down at her.

"You're a cheeky little cow, you are."

He sat on the sofa again and reached for his beer.

"And you," he said to Mam. "Think I won't do it? I will do it. I'm going now. Straight after this drink."

Half an hour later, while Skinner was snoring, Mam eased the beer glass from his hand.

"Can I go out for a bit?" said Vonnie.

"Don't be long, then. It'll be dark soon."

With her denim jacket buttoned right up to her neck over the heavy jumper, and her woolly hat and gloves on, she made her way out of the estate on foot.

Everywhere, the pavements were impacted with snow and ice and she had to walk slowly to avoid falling. The roads were dark grey, mostly clear, but sparkling with a with a sheen of early frost. It wasn't snowing at the moment, but the skies were heavy and grey, creating a false dusk. Not a single other person was about.

The windows of the shops along Main Street were shuttered or in darkness. There was no telling where the pavement ended and the road began: the kerbs were buried under the continuous piled mounds of grey slush.

126

A smooth whirring noise caused her to stop and turn. Along the middle of the grey band of road came a figure on a red bicycle. As the rider got closer, she saw that it was Matt. He almost went straight by, but then saw her and slowed down and stopped.

"Vonnie," he said.

"Hi, Matt. New bike, then? Smart."

"Yeah. Centre-pull brakes, five gears, water bottle ..."

She frowned. Why was he staying out there on the road, with foot-high mounds of filthy slush between them? Why didn't he lift his bike over and come to stand with her?

"Where's *your* bike?" he said "Is it bust?"

"No. I just prefer to walk sometimes."

Matt shrugged.

"Yeah," he said. "I hope you're having a good Christmas. It's crazy at ours. We had this massive turkey. Loads of rum over the pudding and set fire to it. Tins of Quality Street. Booze everywhere. Dad's just about had the whole street in for drinks. A bit canned-up myself."

Vonnie laughed.

"I heard about your dad's big win. It's great."

"Yeah," said Matt. "I'd better go anyway."

He rode off, and she was alone again in the empty street.

20

The Thaw

Snow and ice hung around for the rest of December and the whole of January. There was a lot of talk on TV about American military action in North Vietnam, and Matt hoped that the world wouldn't be blown to smithereens just yet – not before he'd had the chance to snog Dawn Hagley. Jenny moved to London and Matt thought he probably missed her. Apart from playing out in the snow, his next favourite thing was standing at Jenny's bedroom window with the lights off, watching as the snow fell and settled in thick luminous layers across all the back yards.

High winds blew it about in big drifts and he enjoyed helping Dad shovel it away from the doorstep.

Nidge and the rest of the gang still teased him on and off about the night in the woods with Vonnie, but nobody knew anything about the kiss. And Matt had trouble understanding his feelings for Vonnie. He just didn't know what to say to her any longer.

One evening, a water pipe burst in the outside toilet. After fixing it, Dad squatted by the red glow of the fire in the grate as the news came on.

"*... and in Uganda, General Idi Amin has led a military coup and apparently seized power while President Obote attends a summit in Singapore.*"

"Idi Amin," said Dad. "A bad 'un, he is."

He grabbed the coal-scuttle and emptied a load onto the fire. The dust sparked and crackled for a moment, then the fire went dark and smoky. He took an old newspaper from the stack on the floor and unfolded a single sheet.

"Can I do it?" said Matt, leaning forward.

Dad ignored him and stretched the newspaper sheet across the fire mouth, using the flat of his hands to trap it against the brown tiles either side. There was a satisfying sound of rushing air as the fire began to draw. Matt watched as a steady glow behind the newspaper became brighter and brighter. Flames licked up behind, then the newspaper sheet began to turn brown in the middle and Dad released it. The flames consumed the paper and threaded up, yellow and orange, from the coal; they burnt for a short while, then died down again. Dad reached for another sheet of newspaper.

"Can I do it?" said Matt.

"Go on then," said Dad.

Matt slid off the settee, took the newspaper sheet and squatted in front of the fireplace. He stretched the paper across the opening in the tiled face of the hearth.

"Don't be frit of it," said Dad. "Move closer. Get your hands near the top corners. Block the top right off. No gap. That's it. Now get your knees into play. Use your knees to trap the bottom corners. That's it."

Air drew through the remaining gap near the grate, and Matt smiled at the low steady roaring sound. Very soon the flames leapt up behind the newspaper again. A brown patch appeared in the middle of the paper and quickly expanded. Matt grinned. He held on until the last instant, fascinated, then let go and jumped back as the newspaper burst into flame. In seconds, it was reduced to black ashes and went floating up the chimney.

"You've singed hair and eyebrows now," said Dad with a chuckle. "I can smell it."

Most of the snow and ice had melted by the end of January, and Nidge had called for a meeting on Sunday the 31st. From across the town came the tolling of bells from at least two different churches. In Blackthorn Woods, the trees were bare and dark against a blue sky, and the air smelled crisp and musty. The seats were too wet to sit on, but the gang members were busy watching Winston clamber up into a big oak at the edge of HQ. He had a bundle of red gingham material under one arm.

"I had to sneak it back out of the dustbin after Dad threw it away," he called down.

"If this works, it'll be brilliant," said Matt.

"It does work," Winston called down.

The others watched and waited as Winston shunted his way along an overhanging bough twelve feet in the air. He looked shaky as he raised himself to a standing position and arranged the folds of the tablecloth behind him.

"Watch this," he said, gathering the strings in his hands.

Winston jumped. The "parachute" snagged on some twigs and didn't open properly. He hit the ground hard.

"Ow ow ow," he cried. "Ooh ya cow!"

Winston clutched his ankle and gritted his teeth. He stood up and hobbled about.

"Me next," said Badger, reaching for the tablecloth.

"Hold on," said Matt. "There's a better tree at the edge of the Arena. It's got that big branch that's broke. You can get right out to the end of it with nothing else in the way."

"Yeah, that's why it went wrong," said Winston. "You need space around you. It was magic going off the shed roof at home. Till Dad said it was too dangerous."

Nidge pushed his glasses up onto the bridge of his nose.

"Forget the Arena," he said. "We'll go to my house. We've got a long flat roof on the kitchen extension at the back. We can take a run up. Nice soft landing on the lawn."

"What, will they let us?" said Rick.

"I can do anything I like," said Nidge.

"Yeah, Nidge can do anything he likes," said Matt. "His parents are dead cool."

Fifteen minutes later, Matt was running the length of the extension's flat roof, the parachute flapping behind him and the shingle crunching under his trainers. The trouble was, he couldn't see anything. He'd stood at the end of the roof a little while earlier, so he knew about the frog pond and the rose trellises below, where Nidge's dad was digging. But once you were on the roof, all of that was blocked from view by the roof itself. He could see Nidge and the others way out ahead on the lawn.

The last thing he noticed, before he leaped off the asphalt ridge at the end, was Eddie's smirking face. Matt didn't need to be a mind reader to know that Eddie was hoping for the worst. But Matt cleared the frog pond and the rose garden. The tablecloth billowed and snapped with a healthy sound above him. He sailed out and down, then hit the soggy lawn – only churning it up a little bit.

He rolled over, stood, and smiled.

Badger was already moving in for the next go.

"That was brill!" said Matt. He laughed. "It sort of doesn't really even work. It sort of just slows you down a bit and helps to break the fall."

"I know," said Winston, limping across from where he'd been sitting on the garden seat. "It's great though."

Nidge's dad stopped digging for a moment to thoroughly consider what was going on. He watched Badger scaling the ladder, then swivelled his gaze to follow the arc from the roof to the lawn, an arc that passed directly over the little rose garden where he was working.

"Just be careful of your mother's frog pond," he said, running a hand through his greying ginger beard.

"We will do," said Nidge. "Come on, Badger. Kennedy Space Center to Apollo 14: you're clear for launch."

Matt grinned. Apollo 14 was due to launch tonight.

Badger came flying off the end of the kitchen roof. It was difficult to say what went wrong exactly. Matt thought that Badger had lost his grip on some of the strings. The frog pond was safe, but Badger crashed straight into the rose trellises. An entire panel collapsed forward onto the lawn. The tablecloth settled slowly down on top of everything.

"Oh, dear," said Nidge's dad.

Matt and the others went to investigate.

When they dragged the tablecloth aside, Badger sat up, his eyes wild and his face clenched against the pain. Along with the trellis, two of the climbing rose-bushes were wrecked. One was still sticking into Badger, although he seemed unaware. It looked as if his legs had been mostly protected by his jeans, but when he pulled his jumper and tee-shirt over his head, there were a multitude of gashes on his chest and stomach. There was a lot of blood.

"Sorry about the roses, Mr Wharton," he said.

Nidge's mum had come out to the garden now. She'd left the French doors open and George Harrison singing 'My Sweet Lord' spilled out from the radio.

"Oh," she said, seeing Badger. "This is rather ..."

Mr Wharton glanced up at the kitchen roof again.

"Yes," he said. "It is, isn't it?"

"Shall I get the first-aid kit, Dicky?"

"Hmm ... well, I don't know if ... He's certainly hurt."

"Yes. I think ... warm water and TCP to begin with ... um, and then ... bandages?"

Badger swabbed at the blood flow with his tee-shirt.

"He needs stitches," said Nidge. "You'll have to get him to casualty at the Royal."

"I think Nigel may be right, Sally," said Mr Wharton. "I'll get the Cortina started, shall I? The choke's been playing up, but we should all right."

Badger was popular all day at school on Monday, and took every opportunity to show off his seventeen stiches.

That evening, Matt was in the living room watching telly. *Timeslip* had just ended and the news had begun. In his armchair, Dad had a mug of tea in one hand and a Park Drive in the other. On the wall above him was the framed cutting from the *Blackthorn Herald*. It pictured Dad with a gurning smile, holding up his £500 cheque.

Matt watched the recap of Apollo 14's successful launch of yesterday, and the progress report. But when Edward Heath came on the screen to talk about his next move in the Post Office strike, Matt got up and switched over.

A familiar jingle assaulted his ears: *"Decimalisation ~ Decimal-ise ~ Decimalisation ~ Decimal Five."*

He was all for decimalisation, but wished the remaining two weeks were over so that everybody could get on with it and not have to put up with the jingle any more.

In spite of himself, he found his attention wandering to the screen. He pulled a face at the same old grocery items on the counter, the same old words of the shopkeeper.

"That's ten-and-a-half new pence, please."

"That's ten-and-a-half new pence, please," he mimicked, wagging his head from side to side and going cross-eyed.

"What are you doing?" said Dad. "Switch back over. I wanted to see the news."

"Uh, sorry, Dad."

It was still coverage of the postal workers' strike, and Edward Heath was saying that the government's policy to restrict union power would continue.

"Nah," said Dad. "Not a chance, me old china. You'll have to give 'em a rise in the end, like you did with the dockers last summer. Up the workers! Eh, Matt?"

"Yeah. When are the railways going on strike?"

"Dunno. Not yet."

Matt went out to the kitchen. He'd already had his tea but was hungry again. He got the bread and some other things from the pantry and sat at the Formica-topped table. Mum was scrubbing a saucepan at the sink.

"I'll make you a drink in a minute," she said.

While Matt ate, he leafed through an American comic-book, a special edition about the origin of Iron Man. It was so good that as soon as he'd finished it, he went back to the beginning and started again.

There was a knock at the door.

"Oh, here they are," said Mum.

"Wha ...?"

He looked up to see who it was, and was instantly plunged into a state of controlled panic.

It was Dawn and, presumably, her mum. Matt was painfully conscious of still being in his school trousers and school shirt. He thought Dawn looked gorgeous in her jeans and a pink jumper. Her green eyes sparkled and her lustrous dark hair fell about her shoulders.

"Hello, Jan," said Mum. "I told Mathew. Didn't I, Mathew? Told you I worked with somebody at the factory whose daughter was at the Modern School. Do you two know one another?"

"Er – "

"No," said Dawn.

Jan Hagley looked scandalised as she took in the mess Matt had made on the kitchen table with a cup of Bovril and a fish-paste sandwich. She gave him a smile as brief as the flick of a newt's tongue, and turned her attention to the flaking paintwork.

"We'll be decorating soon," said Mum with a hint of the voice she used on the telephone. "Now then, Jan. A nice cup of tea?"

Matt became aware of the Iron Man comic-book in his hands and whisked it under the table. He faked a coughing fit to cover the fluttering of the pages.

"What's that you were reading?" said Dawn, striding forward. "Why have you thrown it on the floor?"

"It's nothing. A newspaper. An old one. Last week's."

"Can I see it?"

"No," he said. "I mean, there's no point. It's just an old newspaper."

"It looked like a comic to me."

She started to crouch down to look under the table. Matt slid off his stool, hooked the comic with his foot and trapped it against the skirting board.

"Suit yourself," said Dawn, standing up. "I don't read comics any more anyway."

"It's not a comic."

"Sit down for a minute, Jan," said Mum. "I'll put the kettle on and mash a pot of tea."

"It's all right, Dot. We won't stay."

"Ooh, I thought you were staying for a cuppa. See to Dawn, Mathew. Get her a glass of squash and get the biscuit tin out."

"Please don't bother with tea," said Jan Hagley. "I'll just borrow those books and – "

"I don't like squash," said Dawn. "Have you got any raspberry cream soda?"

She pulled out a stool and sat down.

"Dawn ..." said Jan Hagley.

Shunting himself down the wall, Matt folded the comic inside his shirt, went to the pantry and threw it on the top shelf. He took the biscuit tin back to the table.

"Sorry, dear," said Mum. "We've just run out of pop. How about something hot? Bovril's nice."

"I don't like Bovril either, thanks," said Dawn, adding to Matt quietly, "It tastes like sick."

Matt flipped the lid off the biscuit tin.

"Are these rejects from the factory?' said Dawn.

"Yeah," he said, taking out a broken chocolate digestive.

"We get them as well," said Dawn. "Ours are better than yours, though."

"No squabbling," said Jan. "A funny age, isn't it, Dot? I can't believe she's twelve on Friday. We're having a party but she only wants girls. When's Mathew's birthday?"

"April. April the 1st."

Mum nipped into the living-room and came back a minute later with a stack of romance novels.

"How can yours be better than ours?" said Matt.

"Don't know," said Dawn. "They just are. We get more chocolate ones. Maybe because Mum's a supervisor."

"I can have any biscuits I want now," said Matt.

Dawn shrugged.

"We're rich," he said. "These are all we've got in at the minute, but we can get anything. Had a whole packet of Jaffa Cakes to myself yesterday."

"Mathew," said Mum. "We're not rich. Five hundred pounds is a lot of money. But it doesn't make us rich. Not at the rate your dad's spending it anyway!"

"We can still buy any biscuits we want, though," said Matt. "Instead of this old reject crap from the factory."

"Mathew!"

"Yeah, soz. I just mean we've run out of posh biscuits."

He noticed that Dawn was looking at him closely.

"Is it really the 1st of April, your birthday?" she said, laughing into her hand. "Fancy having your birthday on April Fools' Day!"

"I prefer it," he said casually, though he was fuming inside. "Anyway, there's loads of chocolate biscuits in here. If you look for 'em."

He raked the biscuits around with his hand, fished out another piece of chocolate digestive and offered it to her. She took it and smiled. When she'd eaten it, she thrust her hand in the tin as well, laughing. And for about five minutes they were both engrossed in searching and eating, until it became a race to find the last bits of chocolate biscuit and they were laughing and scrabbling vigorously in the tin at the same time. Crumbs and fragments flew across the table.

"Mathew," said Mum. "Careful, please."

Matt stopped, and there was a moment of looking into Dawn's eyes and of her looking back.

"Come on, now," said her mother. "We'd better be going. Thanks again for the books, Dot."

Dawn stood and turned away, her long dark hair shining like silk on the back of her pink jumper. Matt was left with the mess of biscuit crumbs and spilt Bovril, and obscure worries about Iron Man.

"See you around, Dawn," he said.

"Yeah," she said, turning back. She tilted her head to one side, and gave him a flirty little moue. "See ya."

Matt's heart pounded.

When they'd gone, he went to the Best Room and stood in front of the big tarnished mirror. He examined his chin from different angles; he ran a tidying hand through his mousey hair; he flashed a smile at himself.

The wonder of him.

21

Freight Train

Vonnie's twelfth birthday was on the 27th of January. She got the record vouchers she'd asked for and went straight out to buy the album *T. Rex* by T. Rex. She played it over and over in her bedroom and sang along.

One day we changed ...

The lyrics ran through her head wherever she went.

She was glad to see the snow finally gone by February. It meant that she could take all her usual short cuts across the Twicken and through the woods without having to wear wellingtons. The trees were static and bare, but it was staying light longer in the evenings. One evening, she stumbled across Matt's lost claw-hammer and took it home. She stashed it at the back of the kitchen worktop, meaning to take it to school for him, but kept forgetting.

She'd hardly seen Matt at all. He hung around in the places at school where he had a chance of seeing Dawn, but whenever Vonnie came to mingle with Nidge and the others at breaktimes, Matt tended to sidle off.

The middle Saturday of February, after an extended night shift at the hospital, Mam brought fish and chips home for lunch. It was Vonnie's favourite.

Skinner settled himself at the table. He hadn't been drinking yet today, but he was miserable and grumpy and had a face like a slapped arse. After eating his battered cod with his hands, he gathered up a swathe of the tablecloth and wiped them thoroughly on it to get the grease off.

"Bill ..." said Mam.

"What?" he said with a dark look.

"Nothing."

Vonnie sprinkled extra salt over her food, and then reached for the vinegar. Vinegar bottles usually had a plastic sprinkler insert in the end, but this new one was different. There was no sprinkler – just an open neck. Vonnie had tipped it all over her dinner before she realised, and her plate was now swimming with vinegar.

"You'll still have to eat that," said Skinner.

"I know," said Vonnie.

She drank the rest of her lemonade and then carefully drained the excess vinegar from her plate into the glass.

"What do you think you're doing?" said Skinner.

Vonnie stared at him.

In her head, Marc Bolan sang, *One day we changed* ...

"Oh, I'm sorry," she said with deliberate sarcasm. "We can't waste it, can we?"

She stood, picked up the glass of vinegar and began to drink. Part way through, she paused and smiled at him.

"Mm, that's nicer than you might think."

"*What? what? what?*" he said.

"Billy ..." said Mam.

He shot to his feet and everything rattled on the table.

Skinner came around the table towards Vonnie and she put the glass down and backed away to the hall door.

"Don't you dare touch me," she said.

"Billy ..."

Skinner kept advancing, so Vonnie backed along the hall towards the stairs. He shadowed her every move, bearing down on her like a locomotive. Before she knew it, she was in between the coat-stand and the front door, with Skinner looming over her, his eyes manic.

"Yeah?" he said. "Yeah? Got something else to say?"

"Bill. Billy, please. She's just a kid ..."

"Keep out of it, you."

Vonnie quaked inside and her heart raced. Skinner was blocking the route to the stairs and she had no idea what he might be capable of doing next. She snatched her denim jacket from the hook and opened the front door.

"Yeah, good move," said Skinner. "Get out."

"Billy, please ..."

Vonnie backed into the porch.

"Er, my shoes," she said.

"Here," said Skinner, grabbing her trainers from the floor and throwing them into the porch. "Come back when you've remembered your manners."

Just before the door was shut in her face, Vonnie heard Mam call out, "Don't be long. It'll be dark soon."

Vonnie put her trainers on and went to the front gate. She couldn't believe the matter-of-fact way that Mam had spoken, as if Vonnie were just nipping out for a nice walk. Did she really not get that Skinner had just kicked her daughter out of the house? Did she really not get that he was an evil pig-dog who shouldn't be allowed anywhere near other people, especially not women or children.

She turned back and saw that Mam was standing at the front window. Mam smiled sadly, in a way that Vonnie imagined was supposed to offer support and love. So why was she staying inside like a prisoner while her daughter was railroaded out of the house?

But Vonnie knew the answer.

One day we changed ...

Mam wanted to pretend that nothing had happened. Wanted to believe that Vonnie would simply come back in an hour and that they'd all just carry on as normal. She smiled back at Mam and raised a hand in a broken wave, then turned and made her way out of the estate.

... from children into people ...

Vonnie didn't know where any of the freight trains went on their journeys beyond Blackthorn. Neither did she care very much. She was sitting on the grassy slope of Gallows Hill. All she knew was that the trains on the track closest to her were leaving Blackthorn and the trains on the other side were on their way into Blackthorn's freight terminal. So far, there had been two trains, and both had creaked and groaned their slow way in the wrong direction.

Over the railway tracks, by the hedgerow to one side of a bare winter field, she saw the old barn that Matt had talked about. She wondered if the owl had its nest there, and would love to have seen it fly overhead again.

Her heart fluttered as she heard a distant chug and squeal. It was another train. And this one was definitely coming from the right direction.

She moved forward, crouched low in the grass and waited. When it came into view around the bend of Gallows Hill, the sight of it caused Vonnie to catch her breath. It was huge and suddenly very noisy and close to her. The engine was brown and dirty and box-nosed, and quickly roared past leaving a powerful smell of diesel smoke in its wake. The trucks were steely grey V-shapes.

Vonnie hurried to the bottom of the hill and onto the narrow band of stone chips beside the track.

One day ...

She was instantly in heavy shadow with the huge trucks towering above. There was just no way that she'd be able to climb into one; she'd have to get onto the chassis first. Cold metal and the stink of grease were all about her. And as slow as the train was moving, the grinding, clattering and screeching was shockingly loud.

Seen from a distance, or from the slopes of Gallows Hill, the freight trains always seemed to be crawling along. Being up close like this, Vonnie realised that it was an illusion. She had to jog to keep up.

Her trainers crunched over the stone chippings.

She reached out and grappled at the cold iron-work, but it was impossible to get a good grip on anything.

Then she tripped over the end of a timber sleeper. For a second, she thought she'd gone under the train. But she was lying on the stone chippings at the side of the track, with grazed palms, watching as the last of the trucks went by and trundled off around the bend.

Half an hour later, as dusk settled over Blackthorn, a steady rain began to fall. Vonnie had been walking past the driveways to the big houses on Fairfield Way. Now she stopped and took the folded paper from her jacket pocket again. 200 Fairfield Way. And there was a number 200 on a wooden post beside the hedge.

It was a long driveway, with two cars parked near the house. Lights were on in the upper and lower windows.

In the open porch, she stood for several minutes looking at the front door. It had a round window divided into stained-glass panes and there was a push-button bell. She kept looking at the bell and looking at the metal knocker. Her heart beat fast. She stepped out of the porch again and approached the bay window. Though it was nearly dark, the main curtains hadn't been drawn yet, and without going too close, she was able to make out three female figures inside. One standing, two sitting.

Flashes of the huge freight trucks came back to her. The deafening noise and the smell of grease and cold metal. She knew that what she'd attempted had been crazy, dangerous and stupid. She could have been hurt. Killed.

Suddenly, Magda was at the window.

Vonnie backed away, confused and a little ashamed of being caught looking in. But Magda smiled, then came out to the front porch.

"Vonnie," she said.

"Oh, er, I'm sorry, Miss Kovacs."

"It's very wet out here. Are you coming in?"

Vonnie glanced towards the window.

"It's all right," said Magda. "You don't have to meet the others. There's a conservatory at the back where we can talk. Are you in trouble?"

Vonnie shook her head and took a step backwards, her nerve and confidence melting away. In her thoughts, Skinner said, "... *straight to borstal, I'll see to that.*" Mam's words came back to her as well: "... *our personal business ... Who is this teacher? I'll go straight to the school and give her a good talking to.*"

"Sorry, Miss Kovacs," she said. "I made a mistake."

She walked away a few steps, then looked back.

"Are you sure?" said Magda.

Vonnie was torn. Miss Kovacs had such a nice smile.

"Yes," said Vonnie. "Thank you."

She retraced her steps out of the driveway and walked back to Main Street in the rain.

> *... The old woman took the sign from Agata's neck and tossed it in her fire. Agata laughed and said that the sign couldn't be destroyed.*
>
> *As ever, she fell into a swoon.*
>
> *When she awoke, there was no sign around her neck. She was no longer sitting by the old woman's fire, nor even on the island, but back on the shore of the lake. She looked out across the lake and there was no trace of the old woman's island, just a flat plane of water to the opposite shore.*
>
> *Agata hitched her knapsack on her shoulder and began walking. She understood that she would never have to wear a sign again, and, deep within herself, something meaningful was stirring.*
>
> *From that moment on, Agata felt as if a fresh cool breeze were blowing through her. When she lay under the whirling cosmos that evening, she sensed a message deep within herself. It was a feeling that had no words, but if it did have words, the words would have been: I SEE.*

22

Vision

Vonnie was squelching along Main Street when a car began to hoot at her. Across the road, the metallic-bronze Zodiac had pulled into the kerb. Skinner had the window wound down and was beckoning for her to cross over.

She stared at him blankly. Why would he think that she'd ever want to speak to him or see him again?

"Come on," he called. "Your mother asked me to come and look for you."

Vonnie stood by the kerb. She was completely drenched; her clothes were wet and cold and clinging to her.

"Come on," called Skinner.

He squinted as the rain angled down into his face. After a few more seconds, he wound the window up. Vonnie thought he was going to drive on, but he turned the engine off and the lights off, and sat waiting.

For another minute, she didn't move; then she crossed to the opposite pavement and stood by the passenger door of the Zodiac, but made no attempt to get in.

Eventually, Skinner leaned over and wound down the passenger window.

"You coming?" he said. "I've been driving everywhere looking for you. Your mother asked me to find you. I've even been to that car on Shady Lane."

He operated the door catch from inside and pushed the door outwards. Vonnie hesitated.

"I'm wet," she said. "The seat."

"It'll wipe down."

Vonnie got in and shut the door.

"I had to come out for some petrol anyway," he said as he engaged the gear lever and pulled away. A hundred yards on, he indicated to turn into the Esso garage.

"Your mother's been worried."

"Has she?" said Vonnie, staring ahead into the rain, and determined to only ever speak to him again in as few words as necessary.

"Yeah. What are you going to say to her?"

"Nothing."

Skinner snorted with laughter.

"What's up?" he said. "Cat got your tongue?"

"Yes."

He laughed again and said, "Right. I'll fill her up with Four Star, I reckon. What's – where did *he* come from?"

A red Vauxhall Viva had pulled up at the pump he was aiming for. All the other pumps were busy.

Skinner thrust his door open and yelled out.

"Oi! Come on, mate. I saw that space first."

The man got out of the Viva and looked over.

"Yeah, you," said Skinner, getting out onto the forecourt and standing with his hands on his hips. "I was here first."

Vonnie wasn't taking too much interest, but she noticed that the other driver was short and quite weedy-looking. If he'd heard all the bar-room brawl stories she'd heard over the years, he'd probably just let Skinner go first. Skinner was big and muscly, and had a mean face.

But the little man swaggered across the forecourt. He was a head shorter than Skinner, but seemed fearless.

"What did you say, pal?" he said.

"Er, I thought I saw that space before you. That's all."

Vonnie could hardly believe what she was seeing and hearing. Skinner had slunk back, and his voice was sounding almost apologetic.

"Think you're a hard nut, do you?" said the other man.

"No. No. I'm just saying ... you know ... fair's fair."

The man looked Skinner up and down.

"You want to make something of it, like?" He took a step closer and jabbed his index finger into Skinner's chest repeatedly. "You want to make something of it?"

"Look, mate. It's a misunderstanding – "

"I'll take your head off."

"What? No, see ... " He glanced back at the Zodiac. "No trouble, eh? I've got a kid with me. Yeah, and ... the doctor said my heart's not too good neither ..."

Vonnie frowned. It was the first she'd heard about that.

The weedy man reached up and gently slapped Skinner across the face. It wasn't even a slap. It was more like a friendly pat with no force or aggression behind it.

"Ya big baby," said the man. "Go on away with you."

Skinner shrank back to the Zodiac and got in.

He reversed and got hooted at by somebody on their way in. When he'd manoeuvred the car out of the garage and drove on a hundred yards, he pulled over to light a cigarette. Vonnie saw that his hands were shaking.

"Are you all right?" she said. "Is it your heart?"

"*What?*"

Skinner's big hands fumbled with the cigarette packet and lighter and they fell to the floor. He scrabbled about to pick them up. Eventually, he got a cigarette lit.

"Not a word of any of this to your mother," he said.

"Doesn't she know about your heart then? She's a nurse. Maybe she could – "

"Shut up about my heart. There's nothing wrong with it. I had to say *something*, didn't I? You could see the bloke was a psycho. Probably just escaped from the nut-house."

Vonnie felt strangely calm.

"I thought you would have just punched his lights out," she said. "You know ... *bosh! bosh! bosh!*"

Skinner gave her a long, deranged look.

"Shut up about everything," he said.

"The rain's almost stopped now," she said, reaching for the door catch. "I think I'll walk the rest of the way."

146

"Yeah, you do that. And not a word about any of this."

Vonnie got out of the car, shut the door, and continued walking along Main Street. The shops were all closed and the yellowish glow from the streetlamps was reflected on the wet shiny grey of the road and pavements. Overlaying the stink of exhaust fumes were the fresher smells of wet concrete and wet tarmac.

She'd only been walking for a few minutes when Matt appeared on his bike. He mounted the pavement beside her, got off and smiled.

"Hi, Vonnie," he said. "I'm glad I saw you."

"Hi, Matt. How's it going?"

"Yeah. Good. I wanted to ask you something ..." He took a peach-coloured envelope from inside his coat and kept passing it from one hand to the other awkwardly.

"What's that?" said Vonnie.

"It's a Valentine's Day card."

"Oh ..."

Matt quickly shook his head.

"It's not for you. Sorry, Vonnie."

She laughed.

"What?" said Matt. "I said I'm sorry."

"It's not that," she said. "Okay. Let me guess. Is the card for Dawn Hagley?"

"Er, how did you ...? Anyway, I was going to ask ... I know she lives on the Willowbank Estate. But do you know what street? And what number house?"

"No. I don't know."

"But you're in her class."

"I still don't know where she lives."

"It's Valentine's Day on Sunday though. Tomorrow. And I can't ... Well ... can you give it to her for me? I mean, take it to school on Monday and give it to her? Don't say who it's from though. Maybe just slip it into her bag or pocket or locker or something?"

Vonnie laughed again.

"I can't believe it, Matt. We were in the woods together that night. Had fun. Okay, got into trouble as well. The police and our parents. But I thought we were friends?"

"Er, yeah. We are."

"Matt," she said. "You've been avoiding me. Why?"

"I don't know. You didn't want to kiss me anyway."

"That's got nothing to do with being friends. Has it? And, anyway, *you* want to kiss *Dawn*. Obviously."

Matt shuffled his feet and looked away.

The rain had started up again, and Vonnie felt its fresh penetration into her scalp. She took the envelope, turned it over and saw that it was sealed.

"Okay. I'll do it. Have you signed it?"

"No," he said. "You're not supposed to, are you?"

"I don't know."

"Uh, well ... she'll know it's from me."

"Will she?" said Vonnie.

Matt frowned.

"Er, thanks for saying you'll help," he said.

Then he got on his bike and rode off.

Back at the house, the Zodiac was already parked along the side. The garage doors were wide open and Skinner was moving about in the fluorescent light and the shadows.

In the house, Mam was ironing shirts.

"Are you all right, love?" she said.

"Yeah ... groovy," said Vonnie. "Really groovy."

"Oh, look at you! You'd better get some dry clothes on."

Vonnie kicked her soaked trainers off.

"Did something happen?" said Mam.

Vonnie smiled to herself.

Did something happen? No, not really, Mam. Nothing important. Nothing you need to worry about. Pig-Dog kicked me out, if you remember? Then I tried to jump on a freight train and nearly got killed.

"Like what?" she said.

Mam bit her lips.

"Well," she said. "It's just that Bill went out looking for you. He said he'd seen you and you were on your way home. But he's been acting ever so strange since he got back. He's in the garage now. By himself. Drinking. Quite a lot, I think. He's taken the gnomes in there from off the rockery. To strip the old paint off and re-do them. It's not so long ago that he – "

"Mam?"

"Yes?"

"He just got threatened by some weedy little bloke at the petrol station and nearly kakked himself."

"Vonnie! Please. He ... What happened?"

Vonnie told the full story.

Skinner stayed in the garage for the rest of the evening. On Sunday, he spent most of the day working on the gnomes again. When he was in the house, he stalked about aggressively, his dark mood like a fog. Vonnie and Mam went quietly about their own tasks. At meal times, Skinner sat silently, ate, then left the table. And it seemed that he wouldn't or couldn't make eye-contact with Vonnie.

... The next morning, Agata rubbed her face with ashes from the dead fire and set off on her way. She travelled for seven days without crossing the path of a single human. When she reached her hometown and walked along the main street, she noticed two things. The first was that nobody kicked her. The second was that everybody except herself wore a sign around their neck. There were signs of every kind. Many said things like: I WANT; or I WISH; or IF ONLY. Others said: TRYING SO HARD; NOBODY KNOWS; I'M THE BEST; IT'S NOT MY FAULT ...

23

Broken Things

Matt was full of the sense of new beginnings on Monday. Decimals went fully live, and he kept spreading his stash of the new ½p, 1p and 2p coins over his desk, sorting and counting them, and looking forward to spending some of them in the chip shop at lunchtime. Debbie Moyes had already been paid off to palm everyone's dinner cards into the box on her way into the dinner hall.

Even more exciting, though, was wondering what would happen when he came face to face with Dawn. He kept looking out for her everywhere he went.

In between lessons, he took extended routes to the next classes in the hope of spotting her. He hurried through the upper and lower corridors, all over the quadrangle, up and down every flight of stairs, backwards and forward across the bridge over the quadrangle. By the time the final bell went, he still hadn't seen her. It would be easy enough, he knew, to find her walking home towards the Willowbank Estate, but now he desperately needed a pee.

As he entered the nearest toilet, he heard the sound of flushing in one of the cubicles. He hurried over to the chipped and stained porcelain urinal.

Just as he was zipping his flies back up, a large hand clapped him on the shoulder.

It was the Gonk.

Matt was seized by the lapels and shoved up against the adjacent wall. The back of his head made a cracking sound on the tiles. For the next two or three seconds, all that could be heard were the gasps of his own breath and the gurgle of water in the toilet cistern as it refilled.

"Got any rocks?" said the Gonk.

"No. I ain't. Honest."

"Every rock on you."

Matt raised his hands above his head in the customary manner and the Gonk checked through Matt's pockets.

"What've we got here then?"

Matt looked at the creased and grubby little package of a brown-paper bag in the Gonk's hand.

"I don't know," said Matt. "It's not rocks. Been there for ages. Probably an old sandwich."

The Gonk unwrapped the package and took out a floppy, squashed triangle of bread. He peeled the slices apart and peered inside.

"Mm, peanut butter ..."

The Gonk stuffed the old piece of sandwich in his mouth and chewed happily. When he'd finished, he said, "What're you doing in here anyway, Super Chin?"

"A slash," said Matt. "I came in for a slash."

"You're a lying toe-rag. You followed me in here to spy on me, didn't you?"

"No. Course not."

The Gonk pushed his broad pimply face forward and flashed a collection of bad teeth in a sneering smile. As he made wrenching movements with his big hands, Matt heard the sound of tearing cotton. One of his shirt buttons popped into the air.

"I've just had a really good crap," said the Gonk, emphasising each word with an extra yank. "It stinks, don't it?"

"I don't know," choked Matt.

"Get in there and have a good sniff then."

The Gonk hauled Matt away from the wall and kicked open the cubicle door. Matt felt hands slamming into his back, and then he staggered forward and nearly fell. A sudden glare of porcelain flooded his vision.

"I said sniff!" said the Gonk. "Go on, sniff!"

Matt sniffed feebly a few times. There was a strong smell of defecation.

"Well?"

"I can't smell anything," said Matt, hating the whiny tone of his own voice and praying it was the right answer, even though he'd never been religious.

The Gonk grabbed Matt's collar, pulled him out of the cubicle and shoved him towards the door.

"Now get lost before I kick your head in."

Matt headed out of the toilet and found the nearest exit.

He collected his bike from the bike sheds and rode as fast as he could towards the Willowbank Estate.

Before long, he spotted Dawn walking with two friends on Horsefair Road. He recognised them as Elaine Smith and Karen Hetherington. Elaine was just waving goodbye.

Matt followed Dawn and Karen at a distance.

A thrill of excitement ran through him as Karen said goodbye. She carried on further down Horsefair Road and Dawn turned off onto Coppice Road. Matt rode slowly, staying back, but not too far back. He wanted to see where she lived but didn't want to lose the chance of speaking to her before she'd gone inside.

Then, not far along Coppice Road, she was letting herself into a little white-painted gate at one of the semis.

Matt rode out into the open from behind the phone box on the corner. He was going to ride no-handed to impress her, but changed my mind. He could always show her that another time.

"Dawn!" he said, with no idea what to say or do next.

She turned from gateway of the little front garden.

"Oh," she said. "Matt. What are you doing here?"

Matt flashed a goofy smile.

"I came to see you."

He parked his bike in the gutter, using his foot to spin the pedal round and anchor it neatly against the top of the kerb. When he moved away from it, the bike stayed there, balanced and upright.

"Nidge invented that," he said. "Not just anyone can do it. Not without a lot of practice. You have to keep the wheels tight to the kerb and get the pedal dead square and everything. You probably noticed that I didn't even look back. That's because I knew it would stay there."

Dawn smiled faintly.

"I can see for myself what you've done," she said. "You don't have to explain it."

"Er, yeah, I know," he said. "I was just saying that Nidge invented it though."

"My cousin's been doing that for years," she said. "And he's never even met Nidge."

Matt frowned.

"How many years?" he demanded.

Dawn let out a torrent of laughter and rolled her eyes; then her expression became serious.

"What do you want?"

Matt licked his dry lips. Behind her, he saw the movement of the net curtain at the downstairs front window, and pictured Dawn's mother standing behind it spying on them.

It was too awkward. Why was she being so difficult? He wanted to make her laugh; wanted to make her like him. But it was all going wrong.

Dawn folded her arms.

"You don't live anywhere near here, Matt," she said. "What do you want?"

"I ... just wanted to talk to you."

"About what? Why didn't you just talk to me at school?"

"I did try. I was looking for you all day ... Er, I mean ... And then the Gonk had me in the bogs. What it is ... I just wanted to know if you got the Valentine's Day card?"

Dawn smiled faintly again and looked down. When she looked up, there was cold light in her green eyes.

"It was from you?"

There was a loud crash as Matt's bike fell over. He glanced back and saw it lying in the road. The front wheel made a ticking sound as it rotated slowly.

"That shouldn't have happened," he said.

Dawn laughed.

Matt laughed as well. Then he grabbed her by the shoulders and aimed a kiss at her lips. She shrieked and twisted sideways, and the kiss grazed her earlobe.

"Get off me!" she screamed. "Weirdo."

The front door opened and Jan Hagley appeared.

Dawn turned and walked up the path, her dark hair fanning out in a brief quarter circle before settling across her shoulders again.

The weather became drier and unusually warm over the next few days, and Nidge decided that it would be a good time to restart the old Thursday evening gang-meetings.

Matt went the long way around, just to enjoy the ride. On Shady Lane, as he skirted the edge of the woods, a strobe of sunlight and shadow played in his eyes.

A little way ahead, approaching the Austin Cambridge from the other direction, Eddie came into view.

"Hi, Eddie."

"Hi, Matt."

Together they threw their bikes across the wide ditch that was full of stingers, then clambered through the rear door of the car and out of the front door on the other side.

"You never said much about that night with Vonnie," chuckled Eddie. "What happened? I won't say nothing."

Matt considered his answer.

"Not much. We ... snogged a lot. She's a really good snogger. Yeah ... we did some other stuff as well. We were on the back seat together, sharing the blankets. It was great. You can't tell anybody."

"Laying on the back seat together? In the nod?"

"Er ..."

Eddie's dark eyes shone.

"You can tell me *anything*," he said. "I won't grass."

"You'd better not."

"So what else?"

"Er, not much else. Let's get to the meeting."

Eddie rode ahead. When they arrived, he sat on his usual seat, the grey-and-red pouffe, and gave Matt a wink.

"Matt was just telling me ..." he said loudly, getting everyone's attention. "That time him and Vonnie were in the Austin Cambridge together. They were snogging each other's faces off half the night ..."

"Eddie!" said Matt.

"And laying on the back seat together under some blankets, completely in the nod."

Matt shot across from his own seat and pushed Eddie backwards off the pouffe. Eddie laughed.

"In the nod?" said Rick.

"Yeah," said Eddie. "Wouldn't be surprised if ..."

Matt leaped over the pouffe and jumped on top of Eddie. Straddling him, Matt clamped his hands over Eddie's mouth. Eddie was still trying to say more and was laughing at the same time.

"Don't blame you, Matt," said Winston, "Vonnie's dead sexy. Were you still in the nod when the police turned up? You going out with each other now?"

"Everybody shut up!" said Matt. "I never said nothing about being in the nod."

"You were snogging her all night, though?" said Rick.

"Er, well – "

"My big brother, right," said Badger, "he snuck his girlfriend into the house one night, and at about three in the morning, the old man – "

"Everybody shut up about it now," said Nidge. "If Matt doesn't want to talk about it, that's the end of it."

"Nobody can say anything," said Matt.

"That's right," said Nidge. "Gang's honour. Nobody here tonight can say anything about Matt and Vonnie in the nod all night in the Austin."

"But we didn't – "

"Don't worry, Matt," said Nidge. "That's the end of it."

"Yeah, thanks, but – "

"Right ... so ... Gang business. Matt got duffed up by the Gonk in the bogs on Monday – "

"He didn't really duff me up," said Matt, sitting back down on his broken dining-chair. "It was – "

"Rick had 35p nicked off him today by Kev Glover," said Nidge. "But Greenie's behind it all."

"We should just have a big scrap on the playing fields at breaktime," said Eddie. "All of us against all of them."

Nidge looked calmly at Eddie for a moment.

"Top marks for bravery, Eddie," he said. "But there's only nine of us and about twenty-two of them, and nearly all of them are second formers. How do you think that scrap would go?"

"Dunno," said Eddie. "I'd have Greenie myself though. He took a Mars bar off me the other week, then kissed me on the cheek. I'd give him a Glaswegian kiss, if you know what I mean. I'd have had him by now, but he's always got the Gonk and Sturgess with him ..."

Nidge pushed his glasses up on the bridge of his nose.

"I've got a plan," he said.

"What plan?" said Monkey-Breath Mosley.

"Not saying for now. I've been sort of researching it for a few weeks. So ... I want Matt and Eddie to meet me on Saturday night. Just you two. Meet me at the top of Grey Goose Street. Half past seven. Right?"

"Right."

"Right."

24

Lost Cat

By Friday afternoon, the school was buzzing with wildly embellished stories about what Vonnie had got up to with Matt in the Austin Cambridge. It was ten times worse than the days following the event itself. At the final bell, she got her bike from the bike sheds and hurried home.

In the kitchen, Mam told her that Skinner was in a "mood", and hadn't gone to work that day. Something was different about Mam, but Vonnie couldn't decide what it was. They both stopped speaking as Skinner came in from the garage. He'd got blobs of red paint on his hands, so Vonnie assumed he was still repainting the gnomes.

"How much money have you got in your purse?" he said. "I'm going to the offie for some beer."

Mam took her purse from her handbag and began to look through the compartments.

"I've not been in today," said Skinner. "I won't be able to get my wage packet till Monday."

"I know, Bill. And ... let's see ..."

Skinner hadn't shaved for several days. He was swaying slightly and looked half drunk.

"Come on," he said as Mam counted out a 50p coin and some 10p coins on the worktop.

"I'll need to keep some back for my bus fares tomorrow," she said, "and then there's ..."

Skinner was breathing heavily. In the next second, he snatched the purse from her and wrenched it wide open.

"*Oh* ..." she said.

"What?"

"Nothing."

He tucked something neatly into this hand, tossed the purse onto the worktop and left.

"I really wish he wouldn't drive when he's had a few drinks," said Mam.

Ten minutes later, there was a knock at the front door.

Mam answered it, and from the hallway Vonnie heard a man asking about a lost cat.

"A tortoiseshell?" said Mam. "No. I'll keep an eye out for you, though." She turned to Vonnie. "Have you seen a tortoiseshell cat wandering about anywhere?"

"No, sorry," she called. "I'll keep an eye out as well. It might be worth having a look on the Twicken."

The man thanked them and left. At the same moment, the Zodiac pulled into the drive and along the side of the house. Vonnie and Mam were in the kitchen again when Skinner came in the side door.

"Who was that?" he said, fists on his hips.

"Somebody looking for a missing cat," said Mam. "Why don't you sit down, and I'll make you a cuppa."

A strange smile crept over Skinner's face, and he went to stand very close to her.

"You expect me to believe that?"

"Sorry? Believe what?"

"A missing cat?"

"Er, yes," said Mam. "That's what he came to the door to ask about."

Skinner's smile grew stranger.

"You're not dealing with an idiot, you know."

"No, I ... Billy, I don't understand."

As well as being unshaven, Skinner now had patchy areas of stubble appearing on the sides and back of his head. Usually, he shaved his face every morning and his whole head probably twice a month.

"It was a man asking about a cat," said Vonnie.

"Stay out of it, you," said Skinner, not looking at her.

"But – "

"Stay out of it. I'm talking to your mother."

He raised a hand and stroked it lightly across Mam's face, his fingertips pausing around her left eye.

Vonnie now realised what was different about Mam. She was wearing much heavier make-up than usual. And there was a dark area around her left eye that the layers of foundation had failed to completely hide.

"The bloke at the door," said Skinner. "Some ex-patient from the hospital ward, was he?"

"No."

"You were flirting with him left, right and centre when he was staying on the ward? Soapy bed baths? Bit of a fling? Now he's asking you to run away with him?"

"No. Bill. Really, I ..."

Skinner sniffed, then started walking around Mam in the middle of the kitchen, looking her up and down as if sizing up a side of meat on a hook in the butcher's shop.

"The bloke was asking about a missing cat," said Vonnie.

"Go to your room for a little while," said Mam.

"No. The bloke was asking about a cat!"

Skinner turned on her and spoke almost in a whisper.

"Go. To. Your. Room."

He still couldn't look her in the eyes, but his entire demeanour radiated hostility. Vonnie backed off down the kitchen as far as the hall doorway.

"Don't you dare hit Mam," she said, her voice shaky.

He turned his attention back to Mam.

"A patient on your ward at the hospital. That's how *we* met. Now you're doing it again!"

"Bill. I promise you on Vonnie's life, I've never ever seen that bloke before. Not ever. Not at the hospital or anywhere else. Never."

On Vonnie's life? Thanks, Mam.

Skinner seemed to consider what Mam had said. He sniffed again and looked her closely in the face. Then he went out to the car and brought his beer in. He loaded most of it into the fridge, then stood the last one on the worktop and flipped the top off with a bottle-opener.

"Where's this come from?" he said, picking up Matt's claw-hammer that Vonnie had left at the back of the worktop after finding it in the woods.

"It belongs to someone at school," she said. "Been there for weeks. I keep meaning to … It's not yours … Honest."

Skinner scrutinised the hammer, weighed it in his hands thoughtfully, then tossed it to the back of the worktop again and went out to the garage with his beer.

Vonnie had been planning to go for a ride around while it was still light, but she stayed in for the rest of the evening because she was afraid of what might happen if she wasn't there. On Saturday, too, she hung around the house again, worried about Mam.

Skinner skipped lunch and sat in the lounge for most of the afternoon, drinking beer and watching the wrestling on *World of Sport*. Mam brought a plate of sandwiches in to him at one stage.

"You really should try to eat something," she said.

For a long time, Skinner stared at the sandwiches on the arm of the sofa. Then he picked up the plate, stood, and threw it against the wall.

In the evening, Matt, Eddie and Nidge stood together on the pavement by the gate to the pub garden, with Nidge peering through a knot-hole. Although there were other entrances into the building from the street itself, most customers seemed to go in or out through the gate to the beer garden, and every now and then the boys would have to move out of the way.

"Won't be long," Nidge kept whispering. "Their glasses have been empty for ages."

He'd already explained that Greenie came here every Saturday night with his parents and sister. Children weren't allowed in the pub, so they had to sit in the garden and have drinks and crisps brought out for them.

Grey Goose Street was lined with spindly, winter-bare trees. Yellow light from the streetlamps cast everything in a jaundiced hue. The Grey Goose Hotel fronted onto the street with its ornate brick façade and twin gables, and at the corner of the building nearest to the beer garden, there was a round tower, or turret, three storeys high, with windows on every floor and a steepled slate roof.

Not far from where the boys stood, a metal grille was embedded in the pavement, and from this grille wafted the constant and pungent smell of ale.

"Okay, we'll be on in a few seconds," whispered Nidge finally. "His old man's just coming out with a tray."

A minute later, on Nidge's signal, Matt and Eddie flanked him and the three walked into the pub garden.

Greenie and his sister were sitting on a wooden bench, huddling themselves against the cold, their fresh drinks and crisps on a little tin table. All the other seats on the grass were vacant. Greenie wore smart trousers, a silky white shirt and a checked jacket. His sister looked a year or two older. She wore a fishtail parka with a snorkel hood. A few strands of blonde hair hung down the front of the coat, and her grumpy face could be seen peering from the fur-trimmed depths of the hood.

"Cheer up, you two" said Nidge. "It may never happen. Oh! Wait ... It will happen. It's happening now."

A flush spread across Greenie's chubby face. His eyes had their usual tired appearance, but grew more alert as he took in the situation.

"Watcha, lads," he said nervously.

A tortoiseshell cat came out from the bushes and began curling itself around Nidge's legs and purring loudly. Nidge stooped to stroke the cat affectionately.

"Who are you supposed to be?" said the sister. "Dick Whittington?"

Nidge smiled. He picked up the girl's fresh glass of shandy and took a long drink.

"Hey!" she said. "You can't do that."

"I'm doing it," said Nidge.

He drank the rest of the shandy, snatched a packet of crisps from the table and opened them.

Greenie stood and puffed out his chest.

Nidge wasn't tall for his age, and although Greenie was a year older, the two boys were about the same height.

Matt and Eddie took a step closer to Nidge anyway.

Greenie sat down again.

"Dad'll be back out any second," he said.

"No, he won't," said Nidge. "He's only just brought this stuff out. We were watching from behind the gate."

"I'll go and get him," said the sister.

"Shut up and sit down," barked Eddie.

The girl did as she was told.

Eddie helped himself to Greenie's drink. Matt hesitated, then reached over and took the other bag of crisps.

"Soz," he said to the sister. "Your dad can get you more."

"You lot have had it at school on Monday," said Greenie.

Nidge shrugged.

"Monday's Monday," he said. "This is happening now."

When the crisps and drinks were finished, Nidge leaned forward and planted a kiss on Greenie's cheek.

"Have fun, kids," he said, then he turned and led the other two out of the beer garden.

162

25

Claw Hammer

... Agata recognised three men walking along the street towards her from the opposite direction. In the old days, when they'd been boys, they'd taken pleasure in kicking Agata. Now grown men, they gave her curious, wary glances, muttered darkly among themselves and carried on by.

Their signs said: I HATE; I'M AFRAID; and ME ME ME.

Agata wandered the streets of the town reading everybody's signs. She saw people who were best avoided, and she saw people who were potential allies. And although she was no longer young, she understood that this was her true beginning.

She had the power of sight. And only one question remained: How would she use this power?

The mean comments and sneaky giggling were even worse on Monday. In every corridor Vonnie passed through, every lesson she attended, every corner of the playground or playing fields at breaktime – there'd be a group of gossipers exchanging ridiculous, filthy stories about what she had supposedly got up to with Matt in the Austin Cambridge that night in the woods.

All night together ... and he said ... then she said ... then when they'd been snogging for ages, he ... in the nod ... and you'll never guess what she ... then they ... and you won't even believe this but she ... and ...

An intense pressure began to build in her chest. On her way to maths, two girls blocked the empty corridor.

"Here she is," said the tallest. "Vonnie Rivers. The first year who knows how to give the boys a good time."

Vonnie recognised the girls as third-formers – Shaz Brown and Cathy something, if she remembered right.

"Can I come by, please," she said.

Shaz, the tallest, folded her arms.

"We've not finished yet."

"Well, *I* have," said Vonnie, trying to squeeze past.

Shaz pushed Vonnie backwards.

Cathy giggled.

"I *said* we hadn't finished," said Shaz. "I want to know what that boy sees in you. I mean, you haven't even got any tits yet."

Vonnie punched Shaz in the face.

Blood gushed from Shaz's nose. Cathy immediately ducked out of the way and stood against the wall. Shaz clutched her nose and stared at Vonnie in disbelief; the girl's eyes were filled with shock, anger and tears.

Vonnie carried on to her maths class, not looking back, and not even caring if the girls came after her. They didn't. She wondered if maybe she'd punched Shaz a bit too hard, then decided that she didn't care.

Later in the morning, the gossip about Vonnie and Matt was overshadowed by a new buzz. A big scrap at lunchtime between Greenie's gang and Nidge's gang. To begin with the talk was of a massive, all-out clash. Then it changed to a one-on-one scrap between Greenie and Nidge. Vonnie wouldn't normally have bothered to follow everybody to the traditional spot at the back of the playing fields. But she was determined to confront Matt; to ask him why the stories about the night in the woods had started again.

By the time she arrived, the size of the crowd was sixty or seventy. Greenie and Nidge were already circling each other on the grass between the silver birch trees and the metal railings. Their blazers and ties were off. Nidge's glasses were off, too, and he was squinting badly.

"Go on, Greenie," shouted Sturgess. "Have him."

Vonnie saw that the members of Greenie's gang were all gathered on one side at the front and Matt and the others opposite. The main crowd was swelling fast. It wouldn't be long, she knew, before the teachers arrived. The strategy, as always, was that the watchers formed a barricade around that corner of the playing fields, so that it was harder for any teachers to get through and break the fight up before it was over.

"Do him, Nidge!" called Eddie.

Greenie made a sudden rush forward, fists flailing.

Nidge ducked to one side, then threw a punch. The single punch smacked squarely into Greenie's mouth and he fell to the ground with bloody lips and a tooth missing.

The crowd roared.

Then Mr Hurst in a tracksuit and the caretaker in a beige smock were pushing their way through.

"Move!" shouted Mr Hurst. "Move! Out of my way."

Sturgess and the Gonk stood over Greenie, trying to help him up and encouraging him to carry on. Greenie looked confused. Blood was streaming from his nose.

Matt, Eddie, Rick, Badger and the others came forward and took turns to hug Nidge.

"Right!" yelled Mr Hurst, reaching the front. "Let's stop this before somebody gets hurt."

Vonnie laughed along with everybody else. Mr Hurst's angry words were meaningless. The fight was all over and somebody *was* hurt. As the jubilant crowd dispersed, Vonne trailed after Matt.

"Hey!" she said.

Matt turned to her.

"Did you see that?" he said, his eyes bright. "One punch! Nidge is the best! That was amazing!"

Vonnie shook her head.

"Yeah, I'm glad about Nidge," she said. "But why is everybody talking about our night in the woods again?"

165

"Er ... I don't know."

"You must have *said* something. It was more than two months ago, and everybody had already stopped talking about it. Why would they start again now? You must have said *something* to somebody."

"No," said Matt. "I didn't. I mean ... I didn't say nothing about us being in the nod together."

"But we weren't!"

"No, I know. That's what I just said."

Vonnie was fuming.

"They probably won't be talking about it any more," said Matt. "Not after what Nidge just did."

"I hate you," she said.

"What? Er ..."

He looked suddenly very worried.

"Vonnie," he said. "Sorry. All right? I'm sorry. I might have told Eddie about the kissing, and then he ... he might have told everyone else, and then everything got exaggerated. But ... I ..."

She glared at him.

"Just don't talk to me again, Matt. Don't talk *to* me; don't talk *about* me; don't come anywhere *near* me. Go back to your stupid gang and leave me alone. I've got too much other stuff happening at the minute."

"What stuff?"

"Just stuff. Leave me alone. I mean it, Matt."

"Vonnie ..."

She turned and walked away.

The school week passed, and she avoided all the places where she might be likely to see him. He'd been right about one thing: the gossip dropped off sharply and became concentrated upon the legendary scrap.

One-Punch Nidge.

Vonnie smiled to herself. It was One-Punch Vonnie, too. But there had been no witnesses; the corridor had been empty. Shaz and her mate weren't likely to be bragging about anything. And Vonnie just didn't care anyway.

At home, the evenings were hard. Skinner hadn't been in to work since Wednesday and he'd taken to following Mam about the house. Mam had told Vonnie that he'd showed up at the hospital twice, checking on her.

Sometime in the dead hours of Friday night, Vonnie was trapped in the throes of a nightmare. She knew she was dreaming but she couldn't wake herself up. And if she couldn't wake up, she reasoned, then maybe it was real? She was imprisoned in a sealed room at the top of a big house. She couldn't remember her own name. It had been taken from her. Everything had been taken from her. And now the soldiers were coming to finish the job. To march her out to the courtyard and stand her before a firing squad. She'd dared to be different and now she had to pay the price. Heavy boots pounded up through the stairwells of the house. Thundered along the corridors. There was nowhere to hide in the dank room. And no way out except the locked steel door they'd be entering by. There was an open skylight in the roof, but there weren't any handholds or footholds on the high walls. The only way to reach it would be by some superhuman power of crawling up the wall like a spider. The click of tumblers in a heavy lock; bolts being drawn ... Vonnie placed her hands on the wall and the wall vibrated and sang gently beneath her touch. She raised a bare foot and it found purchase on the wall. As the steel door swung open, she scuttled up the wall towards the skylight ...

Vonnie woke, sweating and out of breath in the furry darkness of her bedroom. She ran to the window and opened it, hung her head out and gulped at the fresh night air. Blackthorn Woods stretched to the distance in a dark mass. The thinnest sliver of crescent moon hung in the blue-black sky. A lone frog croaked in a nearby garden. She knelt on the carpet at the open window, her chin on the sill, the nightmare polluting her thoughts, dreading the arrival of Saturday morning.

Mam was supposed to be doing a day shift, but Skinner said, "You're going nowhere today."

He spent the afternoon drinking beer and watching the TV wrestling. He still hadn't shaved. His chin was very bristly and the dark patches of hair growing on the back and sides of his head were longer

Mam brought plates of sandwiches in later.

"Please don't throw them at the wall, Bill."

He laughed sarcastically.

"Well, I'm not eating them," he said. "You've probably put rat poison in them, have you?"

If only, thought Vonnie.

"I'll get my own tea," he said.

He went to the kitchen. Shortly, he appeared in the garden with a half-bottle of whisky. He very rarely drank spirits. Vonnie saw him through the lounge window, pacing about in zigzag patterns. Every few minutes, he'd come onto the patio and peer through the window to check that Mam was still there. Then he'd pace again, slugging the whisky. At one stage, he fetched the repainted gnomes from the garage and set them back on the rockery. He stood looking at them for a long time.

Then he came back inside the house. Vonnie heard him stomping up and down the stairs repeatedly, and heard him rummaging about in cupboards and drawers. She shuddered, but couldn't help feeling a tiny bit excited.

"Is he leaving?" she said.

"I don't know," said Mam. "Maybe. Let's just stay in this room, love. Eat your sandwiches."

Vonnie nibbled at the ham and pickle sandwich, but she really didn't have an appetite.

Skinner had made a big pile of something in the middle of the lawn and he was pouring paraffin over it. Just as

Vonnie recognised some of the items in the pile as Mam's blouses and skirts and slacks and bras, Skinner tossed a lighted match on top and there was a burst of flame. He stood back, drinking from his whisky bottle.

"Er, Mam ..."

Mam came to the window. She gasped. Her face looked suddenly pale and haggard.

Vonnie saw her own denim jacket and some of her other clothes on the fire, too.

"Stay in here," said Mam. "I'll talk to him. I know how to reason with him."

"Do you?"

"Yes," said Mam, missing the sarcasm. "Stay here."

She went out through the hall, the kitchen, and out of the side door and around to the garden. Vonnie watched as she tried to talk to Skinner. Mam didn't attempt to salvage any of the clothes. The flames were high and were being wafted about in the wind. The clothes were already scorched and ruined.

Skinner seemed to listen to Mam for a little while, but then he said something that caused her to retreat.

He didn't follow her; he just watched her go. Grinning, he threw the almost empty whisky bottle towards the house and it shattered across the patio. Then he made his way back up the garden, past the shed and the garage.

Mam was already at the lounge door.

"Quick, Vonnie!" she said.

Vonnie followed her into the hall and up the stairs. They went into Vonnie's room, shut the door and sat on the bed.

"He just needs a bit of time," said Mam. "We'll stay in here until he calms down."

The door burst open.

"You think I don't know what you're playing at?" he said. "It's just a game to you. You're trying to trick me into hitting you again. Come on. Who is he?"

"There isn't anybody."

"Yeah, like you told your husband there weren't nobody when you were mauling all around me at the hospital, after my accident. I should have realised then. Should have realised what a tart you were."

Mam said nothing.

"Yeah," said Skinner. "That bloke that fell off the roof who was on your ward. It's him. That's who came to the door. And you lied and said it was a stranger looking for a lost cat. I'm not stupid. I can see what's going on."

"Bill. I promise you ... The man at the door was a complete stranger. The man who fell off the roof was still in hospital. He had a brain seizure last week and went into intensive care. He ... he died yesterday."

"Lies. All lies."

He left the room and stamped down the stairs. Doors slammed. Vonnie went to the window and saw him pacing around the garden again.

After a few minutes, she put her T. Rex album on.

"What are you doing?" said Mam in a loud whisper.

"I don't know," said Vonnie. "I ... we have to ... He's taking everything from us ... It's, like, there'll be nothing left of us if we don't do something."

Mam was still very pale; she was trembling now.

"Keep the volume down," she said.

The music played quietly as they sat beside each other.

Then Skinner came back into the house. Vonnie heard him walking about in the downstairs rooms, then heard him coming up the stairs again. Her heart raced.

Skinner kicked the bedroom door open.

He had Matt's claw-hammer in his hand.

Vonnie watched in horror as he smashed the record player to pieces. Bits of plastic and wood and metal and record fragments flew into the air. Then sparks and a puff of smoke shot out of the ruptured machine.

Mam began to cry out.

"Billy ... please!"

Skinner ignored her. He picked up the LP sleeve and his mouth twisted into a grimace as he scrutinised the image of Marc Bolan and Mickey Finn.

"Look at them! No wonder her head's so full of crap listening to this muck. Long hair and poncey faces. They look three-quarters drugged up and three-quarters queer."

Vonnie leapt to her feet.

"Well you're three-quarters demented! And I wish you were *four*-quarters dead!"

Skinner came slowly towards her.

"You what?" he said.

Mam hurried to put herself in between them.

"Come on, then," jeered Skinner, waving the hammer about. "I'll take you both on if you fancy your chances."

Mam shrank backwards to the bed, pulling Vonnie with her. Vonnie didn't resist. She knew what she'd seen at the petrol station. He couldn't take that away from her. But at that moment, Skinner was oozing violence and seemed capable of anything. She sat on the bed with Mam again and they hugged one another tightly.

Skinner laughed. He swung the hammer viciously and smashed it into the wall, leaving a substantial hole in the plaster. The he lowered his arm to his side and looked steadily at Mam and Vonnie.

"Yeah," he said. "Cowards, the pair of you!"

He left the room and stomped down the stairs.

26

Marmalade Skies

Matt had tried over and over to talk to Vonnie at school that week, but she'd have nothing to do with him. On Saturday morning, Dad gave him another £5 to treat himself. He spent all day in town. He had a few coffees in Woolworths' café, ate loads of crisps, and bought the album *Led Zeppelin III*. On the bus on the way home, he sat at the front of the top deck and kept using the arm of his jacket to wipe the condensation from the window.

He stayed where he was when it was his stop, and continued staring through the damp window. Eventually, as the bus was skirting Woodside Road, he rang the bell and got off. He didn't know the name of Vonnie's road; he only knew that her garden backed onto the Twicken.

It took him less than fifteen minutes to trudge through the bare trees and leaf mulch of the February woods.

The Twicken was approximately a hundred yards wide – a crescent-shaped band of pale grasses and tufty hillocks that backed onto the gardens of the Foxhollows Estate.

Over and over, Matt tramped past the various broken-down timber and chicken-wire fences, his shadow long and thin in the dying light of sunset.

The semi-detached houses and the gardens all looked similar. Although he didn't have a wristwatch, he knew that it must be after five o'clock because the sun was nearly down. It was dry, but cold, and very few people were out in their gardens. In one, a man was having a small bonfire. In another, a woman was digging a plot of ground. But the houses were too far away to see into the windows, and Matt detected no clues as to where Vonnie might live. On his last passage by the back fences, he saw that the man with the bonfire had been joined by his wife. Further along, the digging woman eyed Matt suspiciously.

He retreated across the Twicken and into the woods.

Ten minutes later, he'd arrived at the Austin Cambridge.

He sat in the driver's seat for a while, fiddling with the gearstick and foot pedals. Then he climbed in the back and out of the door that led onto the roadside verge.

Shady Lane was quiet. A strong wind was picking up, and the horizon over the farmland opposite was streaked with deep orange.

Matt remembered trekking in the woods with Vonnie on the night that now felt so long ago. Remembered how he'd led the way with the orange light from the signalman's lantern. Knowing that the shack was a lie. But feeling so close to her in the shared adventure. And wishing that the moment could last. That they could just keep walking through the wood. Out the other side, and over the hills and fields. Under marmalade skies.

A ragged sound came from Matt's throat. He was shocked to find himself crying and was glad that he was alone. He crouched down in case anybody saw him from a passing car. Tears and snot smeared his face, and he had to use his tee-shirt to clean himself up when it was over.

"Mattie. Hello, Mattie. Can you help?"

It was Mrs Patel, the neighbour, hailing Matt from her front yard on Grebble Street as he arrived.

"Oh ... yeah. Hi, Mrs Patel."

The woman stood at the low brick wall that surrounded the little yard, pushing coins around in her purse. The wind was even stronger. It blew dust and grit everywhere and they both had to squint their eyes.

"What's twenty-five new pence in old money again?" she said. "Is it the same as half a crown?"

"No," he said. "Twenty-five pence is five shillings in old money. There's five pence to a shilling. It's dead easy. Half a crown's twelve-'n'-a-half new pence. And anyway I don't even say *new pence* now. I just say *pence*."

"Thank you," said Mrs Patel. "So ... twenty-five pence is the same as five old shillings?"

"That's it."

"Are you all right?" she said. "You look very sad."

"No. I'm okay."

The wind blew at his back as he walked up the entry. Underpants, shirts and sheets whipped about on the neighbour's clothesline. The yard gate was torn from his hands when he opened it, and once inside the yard he had to wrestle to close it again and get the latch on.

Despite the din of creaking fences, clattering dustbin lids and the moan of the wind, he could hear Elvis singing 'Blue Suede Shoes'.

Inside, Dad was at the living-room mirror, adjusting his bootlace tie. He was singing loudly, hips and bottom moving to the rhythm. The budgie squawked and flapped madly about its cage. Dad's hair had been done in a D.A. and he was wearing a brand-new pair of black leather brothel-creepers and blue drape-suit.

"Thought we might have seen you up town," he said, pirouetting from the mirror. "We was there ourselves this afto. Bit of shopping; coffee in Brucciani's; visit to the hairdressers."

"A wonder it's not been blown out," said Matt.

"Nah," said Dad. "You wouldn't catch me paying nigh on a knicker for a D.A. and then let the wind blow it out. They cut some eyeholes out of a cardboard box for me. What's that you've got? Another LP?"

"It's a Led Zep album."

"Not as good as the king though," said Dad, doing a quick bop in front of the fireplace.

Matt laughed.

"What do you think of the new clobber?" said Dad.

"Yeah. Smart."

The stairs door opened and Mum came in. Her hair was in a ponytail and she wore a lemon-coloured jumper and a wide, pleated, black-and-white skirt.

"You look great, Dot," said Dad. "Really great."

"Oh, Ronnie," she said.

He did some fancy footwork and sang along to Elvis.

"Remember this one?" he said, smiling rapturously.

It was 'Hound Dog'. Mum tossed her head and skipped into the middle of the room. And for the first time in years, Matt saw them jiving – Dad twisting her hand over her head and back again, and releasing her into a spin, her skirt fanning up as she twirled.

"Is that stockings and suspenders you're wearing? It's gonna be a great night!"

Matt looked on in horror, then made for the kitchen.

"Eh, Matt?" said Dad. "Why don't you come out with us tonight? Bring your girlfriend. What her name?"

"Vonnie," said Mum. "She's lovely."

"We're off any minute. Early doors. Taxi's on the way."

Matt had to fight back any more blubbering. There was no way he was going to cry in front of his parents – not when he was only a month off twelve years old. He kept his face turned away from them.

"She's not my girlfriend."

"Come yourself," said Dad.

"I'm not allowed in pubs."

"It's the Working Men's Club. You're allowed in there. Rock 'n' roll group on. Come on. A few pints of shandy."

Matt smiled.

"Yeah. Okay. Thanks, Dad."

It had been quiet for more than a quarter of an hour when Vonnie and Mam crept downstairs. They found Skinner in the lounge, flopped across the sofa, arms and legs flung out. A bottle of Double Diamond stood on the coffee table. His face looked ugly and angular in the half-light. It was difficult to say if he was asleep or awake. His head lolled about and a mumbling issued from his dribbling mouth.

"Mam," whispered Vonnie, staying by the door. "Please. Let's just go. He's going to hurt you. Us. If we stay."

Mam stared at her.

"He can't hurt anybody in this state, love. Anyway, we can't just go. We haven't got anywhere *to* go. We'll try to get him up to bed. A good sleep and he'll – "

"No," said Vonnie.

Skinner grunted and sat upright. He struggled to stand.

"Where's my dinner?" he slurred, eyes out of focus.

"Oh ... are you hungry?" said Mam.

"Where've you been?"

"Nowhere, Bill. I'm here."

He got up and found his beer bottle, had a leisurely drink, then stood swaying, trying to focus on Mam.

"If he's ... put one finger on you ..." he slurred. "I'll kill him ... and I'll kill you."

"Billy," said Mam. "I promise you that – "

Skinner bellowed with sudden rage and kicked the coffee table over. Mam retreated to the doorway. Vonnie was already in the hall, heart pounding.

"Mam," she said.

The only thing that made sense to her was getting out of the house. Now. But she couldn't leave Mam behind.

Skinner staggered about, grunting and shouting. He went to the garden window and tried to open it like a door.

"He barely knows what he's doing," said Mam in a calm voice that was at odds with the fear in her eyes. "We'll nip out for a little walk and give him a chance to sober up."

"You're going nowhere!" growled Skinner.

He lurched away from the window.

Halfway across the room, he tripped over the upturned coffee table and fell to the floor, swearing.

176

Vonnie tugged on Mam's arm, pulling her further along the hall. She scrabbled about at the coat-stand, finding nothing of their own, and remembering the bonfire.

Skinner came out to the hall, but went in the wrong direction, to the kitchen.

"Where are you?" he shouted.

"We have to go *now*," said Vonnie, low and urgent.

"My shoes – "

"Everything's gone."

Vonnie pulled Mam out to the porch and out of the front door. They hurried along the path to the pavement as another crash sounded in the house.

Twenty minutes later, Vonnie was still holding Mam's hand, leading her to the western edge of Blackthorn. A strong cold wind blew at their backs. Vonnie was in just a tee-shirt, jeans and trainers; Mam had a thin blouse on, a skirt and her slippers.

Vonnie kept looking behind, worried about the Zodiac appearing at any moment. Surely he wouldn't be capable of driving? But as well as keeping an eye out for his car, she was alert to every side street and alley that they might use as an escape route.

"This way," she said, as they reached Fairfield Way.

"Oh ..." said Mam, almost in a trance.

"We can't go back," said Vonnie.

"What? We have to."

"No."

Mam stopped walking.

"I haven't even got my handbag. We've got nothing."

"It's now," said Vonnie. "Now. Don't you see? It has to be *now*."

"What has to be now?"

"Please, Mam. You have to trust me. We'll go and see Miss Kovacs. The teacher I told you about."

Mam frowned and shook her head.

"Mam. Listen. We'll go and see her. Just for a little while. A visit. Something. Anything. She's really nice."

Mam walked slowly beside Vonnie again.

"We can't just turn up at somebody's house ..."

Vonnie gripped Mam's hand tighter and kept walking.

"Yes we can. Just to say hello."

"Well ..."

She began to resist again when they were in the driveway of the big house, but Vonnie hurried to the porch and rang the bell. Mam was still standing in the middle of the drive when Magda came out.

"It got really bad," Vonnie blurted.

Magda nodded and gave Vonnie a brief hug. Then she went up to Mam and offered her hand.

"Magda Kovacs," she said.

Mam looked confused and embarrassed, but she shook Magda's hand and tried to smile.

"Brenda Rivers."

"You're welcome. Please come inside and join me for tea. I made a fresh pot a minute ago."

Magda led them through a hallway with a mosaic-style floor. They came out in a large conservatory at the back. A group of wicker chairs were arranged at the big windows for the best view of the garden and countryside beyond. The sun was down in the west and the sky and the undersides of the clouds were tinted orange.

"This is very kind of you," said Mam when the teacups were being handed around. "We were ... out for a walk, and Vonnie said you lived here. So good of you to offer us tea. We'll get going again soon ... Just a walk ..."

She looked at the floor, then noticed with alarm that she was wearing her slippers and tried to tuck her feet out of sight under the wicker chair.

Magda Kovacs exchanged a knowing look with Vonnie that required no words. Mam was an innocent – more a child than Vonnie at that moment. She needed handling

178

gently. And Vonnie understood that they were both safe now. Wherever the immediate future or the longer-term future might lead, they were safe in this moment, and Magda would help them. There would be no going back to Skinner's warped and hostile world.

Vonnie felt relaxed for the first time in ages. Amid all the difficulties of recent months, she'd barely had the chance to think about the biological changes to her own body. She was leaving childhood behind. She still didn't know if she fancied boys or girls, or both, or neither, but she knew that it didn't matter and that she didn't have to decide. There was no pressure. No hurry. There was time enough to discover the answers. Her answers.

She remembered being in the Sick Room with Magda. And of Magda talking about society's shortcomings and how women who were victims of brutal treatment had nowhere to go for help. How a friend in London was trying to set up a special refuge. *Maybe women are the only ones who can truly help women.*

"Lovely cup of tea," said Mam. "We'll get going soon."

Magda smiled.

"Of course, Brenda," she said. "You can go whenever you're ready. But, please ... Rest a while for now. Enjoy the evening. And there's a spare room ... if you felt that it would be helpful to stay the night; or stay longer ..."

Mam looked confused.

"No. We can't stay. I mean ... we hardly know you."

"Take your time, Brenda. Take all the time you need."

Vonnie felt her tired body relaxing deeper and deeper into the contours of the wicker chair. She sipped her tea and looked out over the countryside.

In the west, the sky was the colour of marmalade.

Author's Note: If you have enjoyed this novel, please consider leaving a brief review or comment on Amazon.

Note on bullying and domestic abuse: If you are being affected by bullying or domestic abuse, speak to a trusted teacher, adult, parent or carer, and/or seek support by calling Childline. The phone number is currently 0800 1111. Wider support and advice is available from Refuge and Women's Aid. In the UK, there is a 24-hour national domestic abuse helpline; the number is currently 0808 2000 247.

Printed in Great Britain
by Amazon

57411734R00108